AF574767

A DOG AT HEEL

A DOG AT HEEL

BEATING, PICKING-UP, RETRIEVING

Veronica Heath

THE BOYDELL PRESS

First published 1987 by The Boydell Press
an imprint of Boydell & Brewer Ltd
PO Box 9, Woodbridge, Suffolk IP12 3DF
and Wolfeboro, New Hampshire 03894–2069, USA

ISBN 0 85115 482 4

British Library Cataloguing in Publication Data

Heath, Veronica
A dog at heel. Beating, Picking-up, Retrieving
1. Hunting dogs —— Training
I. Title
636.7'52 SF428.5

ISBN 0-85115-482-4

Library of Congress Cataloging in Publication Data

Heath, Veronica.
A dog at heel. Beating, Picking-up, Retrieving
1. Hunting dogs. I. Title.
SF428.5.H38 1987 636.7'0886 87-9368

ISBN 0-8115-482-4

Printed in Great Britain by
St Edmundsbury Press, Bury St Edmunds, Suffolk

CONTENTS

Introduction

This book is written for amateurs by an amateur and is not intended to be a gundog training guide. Only one chapter is exclusively devoted to training, because there are several good books which already cover the subject better than I can. My aim is to explore the different options open to the novice when he, or she, decides to get a gundog to accompany them either shooting, picking-up or beating. Amateurs helping on shoots today have to be efficient to be acceptable and there is keen competition to join the team on most estates.

I have explained exactly what the work will entail and I hope my readers will be encouraged to get themselves a gundog. They will soon find themselves with an addictive sport which will give years of pleasure, as well as providing a useful and humane service to the shoots concerned.

Veronica Heath

Northumberland.

CHAPTER ONE

A Day to Remember

Leaning on his thumbstick in a dene shrouded with brambles, a picker-up is watching the plantation more than a hundred yards away. As yet no sound breaks the stillness and he savours the moment, alone with his dogs, in this quiet corner of the countryside before the hectic activity of his day begins. To the south, the ground drops away to an undulating pasture of old rig and furrow, while northwards he can see the Cheviot hills already topped with the first snows of the year. This is a private estate on which Tom is made welcome and before he was involved in the shooting scene it would have been unthinkable to find himself in such a place. He can understand how difficult it must be for those not involved in field sports to appreciate his commitment. Whereas when he simply walked in the country he was just a figure on the landscape, now that he is part of the shoot he feels that he has become part of that landscape.

An owl breaks from the covert ahead and Tom watches it flap unperturbed over the guns standing at their pegs in the gulley that drops away in front of the wood. He can hear a steady tapping has begun a long way back and, faintly on the breeze, the startled call of the first cock pheasant to be alerted. Tom's dogs, poised beside him, rise imperceptibly from their haunches and tremble with anticipation, but a hiss restrains them and they sink disappointed, to sit again. They are Teal, a strong black labrador, a seasoned bitch of several years retrieving experience and Mel, a young liver and white springer spaniel bitch which he has trained to the gun himself. This is Mel's first day on a big shoot where there are sure to be cripples to find, with few of the guns having dogs themselves and limited time between drives to use them. Tom can see the guns' dogs pegged beside them, a few held by smart tweeded wives or girlfriends perched on shooting sticks, elegant with bright scarves and painted fingernails. This is a 'let' day on the shoot and the keeper and his team of beaters, stops and pickers-up are all on their mettle to show good sport.

Tom can just see the other picker-up who has been invited to help on the shoot, an invitation only extended to seasoned campaigners of proven ability. A housewife shrouded in wellies and a waterproof jacket standing well back against a wall encircling a small copse, where she knows from experience that crippled travelling pheasants will try to gain shelter. A yellow labrador sits expectantly beside her, savouring the joy of the moment as much as her mistress. The lady originally came along as a beater on the shoot just for the fresh air and exercise but having become addicted, she has graduated to working a trained dog and is now a respected member of the team.

Momentarily, the tapping has ceased, the atmosphere is electric with anticipation. The stillness, the scenery, the wildlife, the wind, even the rain, make up the joy of the day. Cares are cast away and spirits soar as with a clatter of wings, the first cock pheasant breaks from the wood and sails high over the end gun.

With the wind in its tail, the bird coasts on over the danger zone. Two shots crack, but it flies on unscathed. Faintly on the wind, Tom can hear a shout of 'Steady on the right . . .' the familiar voice of the head keeper restraining his team of beaters. Then a single shot rings out and a bird Tom has not seen is suddenly planing down beside him, tilting slightly as it lands and scuttling broken-winged and frantic, neck outstretched to totter to the sanctuary of the brambles behind him.

As the bird hits the ground, Tom knows that he must send one of his dogs to bring it in. Placed as he is, it matters little and the sooner the dog gets going the sooner the pheasant will be in his gamebag. Silently, he lets the labrador slip off – better not risk Mel working until the drive is over. As the dog streaks out to gather the fated cock, two more, and then half a dozen explode out of the wood, and he is marking two on the right, way back, crippled into the brambles, and a third tumbled into the gulley on his left.

Teal gallops in, ecstatic, bird in mouth, her 'raison d'être' complete and Tom checks her momentarily while he marks several more birds swishing down to right and left. Out of the corner of his eye he can see the other picker-up's yellow labrador scaling the wall and dropping down into the copse for a runner. He knows that he must keep Mel on 'sit' until the whistle signals the end of the drive, because the pace is too hot for a young dog and he suspects that she could be distracted by the gunfire. It is surprising how many birds do come over the guns apparently unscathed, and then collapse some way back. Silence is essential behind the line and having sent out Teal to collect, there must be no whistling or signalling despite the fact that she may be ranging too far. The keeper would not be pleased to see his birds running like stags out of the next covert because of a noisy handler. He must put his trust in her ability to retrieve her 'mark' or to locate her quarry by scent.

As a last flurry of birds show over the two end guns, Tom takes a flapping hen pheasant from Teal, without taking his eye off the tense little spaniel poised at his side. Given half a chance, Mel will anticipate a command and be off in a flash. He must always watch both dogs, mark birds, and keep an eye on the covert ahead for the first sight of the beaters. Now a bright yellow mackintosh-clad figure appears from behind a tree and within seconds the whistle goes to signal the end of the drive. Now he lets the spaniel go out and she races off, wildly excited, head up and deaf to his directions so that his heart sinks as he sees his weeks of training forgotten in the heat of the moment. Teal helps by coming in with a crippled bird and as Mel runs to check the trophy in her kennel mate's mouth, Tom is able to get her in. No time now for recrimination; he must leave her initiation for a quieter moment and give her an easy bird with no distractions only when a suitable opportunity occurs.

Five cocks and two hens make up Teal's bag for the drive, and now Tom makes his way quickly over to the game cart and hands the birds over to be racked up. No picker-up can carry that number of pheasants very far. A word exchanged with the lady picker-up to check that all their birds seen down have been collected and then they walk together, dogs at heel, to place themselves for the next drive.

Later in the day Tom gets a chance to work Mel, and, although she fails to pick a dead bird in a root field, he is happy to see her first exuberance wear off. Roots are a spaniel's forte and he had already given her experience in working in them. The dog began to quarter her ground correctly, bustling here and there, nose down, getting on with the job. Unfortunately, one of the gun's sends his dog in too and he finds the cock before Mel does, but later in the day she gets a chance to pick an easy bird in some bracken.

Tom's dogs work three days a week on local shoots during the season, beginning with partridges in September and finishing at the end of January. After several weeks they get fit and lean and with their

Late in the day Tom's young spaniel gets a first chance to retrieve a pheasant

days fraught with anticipation, excitment and intense concentration they quickly react by shedding flesh and muscling up. When Tom bought Mel in as a pup to bring on, it was stamina and toughness that he looked for, as well as brains, nose and style. He is careful not to commit himself to beat or pick-up on more than three estates in the neighbourhood, because dates can conflict. Keepers like a regular team who turn up on time, know the ground and do their job without fuss. Last minute apologies for absence are a headache for the shoot organiser. Top class shoots now have hundreds of birds falling to the guns and without a good team of helpers most shoots could not function.

Efficient amateurs like Tom are now in demand. Shoot costs are exceedingly high and shoot managers need men and women with a commitment to the job who are prepared to work either as beaters or pickers-up as the need arises. It will likely be necessary to have several years experience before a novice can expect to be included in a big shoot like the one described above, and only a seasoned campaigner can expect a really novice dog like Tom's young spaniel to be welcome. Many women now appear regularly in the ranks of pickers-up and in the beating line on shoots. A few get to grips with the job and find the work satisfying and fun. Many drop out, disheartened and disillusioned, and this goes for aspiring novice male handlers as well. In most cases the dog is unsteady, the handler loses confidence and invitations to help do not materialise. It is my intention here to guide the amateur along the right lines to success.

The emphasis in the gundog training field today is on educating the owner/handler as well as the dogs and it is much easier to be successful now than it was when I started gundog work twenty years ago. This book is about dogs who are going to work live game on big shoot days as well as small rough ones and this is different from competing in working tests and field trials. Because the standard is high, so keepers and shoot managers have come to expect first-class work from their amateur assistants. Professional trainers have to handle puppies which clients bring them – we amateurs have the advantage of being able to choose the raw material ourselves.

Join the ranks of the beaters and remain dogless yourself for one season. Watch carefully which are the gundogs you like, which seem to you to respond willingly and correctly, and which owners most nearly correspond to what you hope your role in the field is going to be. The way to learn is to see how other successful amateurs have succeeded. Ask them how they did it and learn from them where to go for a suitable young dog, trained or untrained, whichever you decide is for you. Remember that these lay pickers-up with good dogs are the people you have to emulate, not the professional trainers who handle their dogs with a sharpness and control which you do not need, and are unlikely to be able to emulate. A novice who is prepared to take time to learn will be successful, and will ultimately convince neighbouring keepers and landowners that they would make a good and useful addition to their team.

CHAPTER TWO

What are the Options for the Amateur?

Gundog breeders are now producing puppies with such ability and latent talent that it only requires a trainer to develop these natural gifts of intelligence, nose, mouth and the instinct to retrieve to produce a useful working dog. However, although some novice owners with puppies have been successful at training, I would not recommend it with a first dog. Far too many amateurs have found the high standard now expected in the shooting field is more than they can achieve, or sustain, and the dog has ended up spending most of the day in the field on a lead. The man who carries a gun and must spend much of his day at a peg, only using his dog for close retrieves, needs a rock-steady retriever and I have nothing but admiration for the busy amateur guns who train their own puppies and achieve this. Their requirement is not the same as the man or woman who requires a dog to work in the beating line or to pick-up behind the guns. So we must consider where you are likely to be able to work the dog and what breed is going to be suitable. Watch the gundogs that other amateurs have been successful with, ask where they got the pup, who trained it and for how long.

Dual-purpose gundogs combine the roles of flushing game, retrieving it and even pointing if need be. It may be tempting to consider how useful these assets would be in the shooting field all in one paragon dog, but I strongly advise the novice not to try and train a puppy to do all these tasks or even to take on a trained dual-purpose animal and expect it to remain steady. The majority of steady retrievers are ruined by being allowed to join the beating line and flush birds in front. When I see a new recruit on the team on a shoot with a promising young dog nicely to heel and then witness that same dog bounding joyfully about in the brambles in the beating line, I know that within half a season he will be out of control. The criterion is to resist the temptation to attempt too much with a first puppy. We need a dog which will walk to heel, remain steady to the fall of the bird and then will retrieve on command. It is very nice to see dogs handled by professionals at field trials, but in the shooting field it is not always practical to expect the dog to look for directions and a picker-up's dog must learn to think for itself. There are times when the dog will disappear from sight and we must put our faith in his ability to work out the line for himself and to return at once, successful or unsuccessful, to report to master on the specific job that he was sent out to do. Beating dogs must work in sight of their handler and preferably within thirty yards of him, with an immediate stop on flushing game. I like my dogs to look to me when game is flushed and to pause before plunging off again, so that I can either recall or redirect. It comes down to that invisible thread between dog and master which must never be broken.

There are several options open to us. Either we buy a fully trained two year old dog or a part-trained dog about fifteen months old, used to dummies but still very green on live game, or a ten to twelve week old puppy, either to send away for training or to train ourselves.

The advantage for a novice of buying a fully trained dog is that all the groundwork will have been done and it will just be a question of keeping up the standard of training already achieved. The animal will still be young enough to serve for years and he will teach our novice a great deal about good dog work in the field. It is essential to visit the trainer for several lessons on how to handle the dog. The misapprehension that an adult dog may not settle with a new home and a new owner has proved to be unfounded in almost every case that I know. This is the way I started and I have never regretted making the decision to buy a fully trained springer spaniel. Having watched two different spaniels for a whole season working quietly and consistently, both of which belonged to different owners, I made enquiries as to how the miracles were achieved. They had been beautifully trained by a keeper at Edmundbyers in Co. Durham; so I bought a two year old spaniel bitch from him myself, went up to the moor and had several outings with him, and then brought my new recruit home. We never looked back. She worked for me for many years and taught me enough to enable me to take on a part-trained dog to finish off myself a few years later. Now I can with confidence train on a complete novice provided it is carefully chosen from the right breeding and background.

A part-trained dog could turn out to be well grounded in the basic

A dog to be used for beating work must keep within 30 yards of the handler

disciplines i.e. walking to heel and obedience and work well on dummies. If this is the case, the transition to the real thing should be straightforward, but still quite a challenge for the novice if the dog is inclined to be headstrong or, alternatively, lacks a natural inclination to retrieve live game and needs help. Having had experience with one successful fully trained dog, the amateur should have no difficulties. The secret of a good gundog which remains consistently biddable over several seasons work is solid groundwork in that essential discipline – obedience. If this all-important preliminary has been achieved then you will be over half way to the finished product. It might be as well, however, to tell a salutory tale at this point because I think it does illustrate some of the pitfalls of taking on a half-trained dog and how to make the best of what could turn out a disaster.

A friend of mine got tired of sitting on a shooting stick admiring her husband's expertise and decided that she wanted to get more involved in the scene. They went on holiday to Angus in Scotland and she came back with a springer spaniel. They had bought the dog from one of the resident keepers and called him Angus. He was described as 'half-trained' and coming from such a good keeper he was bound to turn out to be a huge success. All she had to do was to practice a bit on the lawn with her new whistle and dummy and in no time Angus would be retrieving her husband's birds to command, walking to heel and coming immediately she called him.

It did not turn out like that at all. For a novice owner, if the puppy has not been basically well taught, it seldom does. Angus quickly showed his form and became the wildest thing, racing about with his head down after ground game, deaf to whistle and signal. My poor friend ran miles after him and in the end she gave up trying to control him. He barked when she shut him in the kennel, he chewed a mat when she left him in the house and if she took him out on a lead he pulled all the time. He soon forgot about walking to heel. She was in despair and if she could have found a good home she would have given him away.

Fortunately, I know a man who organises dog training classes. He specialises in training gundogs and I had met him picking-up on a local shoot. He has minimal premises and trains on a local common. But watching him work his dogs on the shoot I knew that he had a natural affinity with them. With reliable shooting dogs and trained guard dogs fetching good money today, he has built on his expertise and now has an enviable local reputation. He does not like taking on spoiled young dogs, especially one as wild as Angus, no trainer does, but he agreed to see him.

The man hid a cold partridge in a dyke and gave the dog a chance to see what he could do. Of course Angus rushed about wildly, but he must have sensed that here was a chance for him, because instead of disappearing into the next parish he did stop long enough to wrinkle up his nose and pause to wonder what it was that had been hidden. Anyway, he not only found the partridge but picked it up and came back over a wall in style. Of course he refused to give it up and threw it in the air and then ran off and started to pluck it. But the trainer thought that he did show potential. 'The way he picked that bird he could make a stylish retriever,' he told us. 'If I can get through to him and get him to respect me, I might be able to make something of him . . .'

My friend admitted that she felt handing Angus over to a trainer for several months discipline and training was an admission of failure. But in her case it had been a case of the blind leading the blind. If the trainer could discipline Angus, I urged her to attend his training classes and they could progress from there.

It took my friend and her wayward spaniel many months of regular lessons and homework practising alone at home, but at last Angus has come to respect her and they are beginning to get on together. 'I cannot believe how ignorant I was,' she told me. 'No wonder the dog got out of hand. I have had to have lessons in how to handle him . . .' She paid out nearly two hundred pounds in boarding and training fees for a preliminary three months and then when he returned home they continued to attend regular weekly sessions. At the end of the last shooting season she went with her husband to a small family shoot where she kept Angus at heel and only allowed him three easy retrieves. But she never put the lead on him all day and he brought two of his three birds in to hand in copy book style.

This particular trainer told me that one of his clients is a young army officer. He bought a labrador puppy of good breeding from his kennel and, despite being totally inexperienced himself, the officer wanted to try and train his own dog. 'It was not convenient for him to come to my classes during the day,' the trainer told me. 'So I go to his place every Monday evening and he has a private lesson. They are both learning and the result is going to be a successful partnership which he could not easily have achieved on his own.' Expensive, perhaps, but the pup was not cheap and if the end result is an efficient gundog which will serve him for many years it will be money well spent. 'Most of the training I am doing myself,' the young man told me. 'But I'm getting expert guidance and if he sees a problem developing, he helps me to deal with it at once.'

It is worth remembering that some trainers will not willingly part with a dog described as part-trained if they think it is a good one. A few more months work and, things being equal, the dog might command a higher price. On the other hand, the trainer may genuinely be over-dogged, he may need the money or perhaps the dog is not one with which he can build up a good relationship although someone else might. The moral is to insist on a realistic demonstration with live game in natural conditions. It is easy enough to show a pup off as obedient by stopping it to rabbits in the pen or whistling it in in the seller's back yard. Insist on watching it work where there is game scent and genuine temptation so that you can assess the true potential of the animal. A beginner should take an experienced friend along when he visits the trainer for a demonstration.

Many people like to have a dog from early puppyhood because they feel that it will then integrate better in the family. So a puppy can be bought in at ten weeks old and live with the family until eight to ten months old when it can go away to be trained. With this arrangement, the majority of trainers prefer the owner to do nothing at all with the pup until proper training commences. If the novice is still determined to train the puppy himself with the help of a good training manual then the same rule applies and no field training should be attempted too early. The average spaniel is mature enough to start work around six to eight months and a labrador around eight months old. This is only a guide because individuals differ as to when they mature and one does come across paragons which retrieved like veterans at six months old. Occasionally, however, these same brilliant pupils go to pieces a year later because they have been pushed too early. I did no work at all with my present labrador and she took to work with alacrity at ten months and was in full work on live game at two years old. It must be emphasised here that a puppy must not be allowed to roam and to pick up bad habits, like hunting the hedgerows with other miscreant canine members of the family.

CHAPTER THREE

Choosing a Puppy

The belief that labradors and golden retrievers are steadier and easier to handle than spaniels, is no longer justified. Retrievers are now so highly bred with inherent working instincts that most of them have as much speed as a long-legged spaniel and they are quite as challenging to train. When choosing a puppy for work in the shooting field, I cannot emphasise too strongly that it is breeding which counts. A thoroughbred dog, bought from a long line of disciplined ancestors will almost certainly be the cleanest and the healthiest dog. Quite apart from practical considerations he will also be the handsomest dog. The gundog group, as recognised by the Kennel Club, consists of pointers, setters, retrievers and spaniels. Study the breeds at work in the shooting field and see which appeals to you. Go and look at the gundogs parading at the C.L.A. Game Fair. I love the bustle and drive of the spaniel, many of my friends prefer a labrador, a golden retriever or a flatcoat, being larger and therefore regarded as more use as a guard dog, and labradors have a reputation for being good with children. However, since the working qualities of retrievers, labradors and spaniels have been improved with careful breeding policies designed to increase drive, speed and style in the field, much of the domesticity desirable in a house dog is now absent. I do keep my dogs largely in the house because it suits my lifestyle to do so, but they are equally at home in the kennel. I have working labradors and spaniels and find neither particularly restful on the hearth, they need discipline and a sensible routine. If the idea of a gentle, plodding labrador or golden retriever appeals, and your neighbour has a litter from his bitch which occasionally accompanies him shooting and sits, or rather lies, comatose at his peg on the field, then you will get a pup which will grow into a nice family dog, but it is unlikely to be much use to you on your beating and picking-up forays. With spaniels, it is

Go and look at the different gundog breeds parading at the game fair

necessary to be equally vigilant. You could find yourself with the opposite problem here. There are still some headstrong dogs about which could land an unsuspecting novice with a self-willed pup which proves difficult for the best trainer to teach and subsequently control, never mind an amateur. It is too late when you are half way through your first season on the shoot and having problems with the young dog, to be told then that the sire or the dam was not much use on the field.

So, whichever breed you choose is a matter for personal preference. I have found a spaniel and a labrador make a useful working combination but they take a lot of handling. Stick to one or the other for a year or two. Whichever you choose, check the parentage carefully and if possible see both at work in the shooting field and ask yourself whether they are the type of dog you have in mind for yourself. If you buy from a keeper and you do not know the man, check his credentials, or rather his kennel carefully. Selling livestock is a salutory business and if a breeder sees a possible sale to a good home, he will need to be saintly not to point out any defects in his dogs' pedigrees. To most amateurs, a pedigree form is so much paperwork and illustrious names with Field Trial abbreviations after them should not give the novice false ideas about the puppy's trainability. However good his breeding he will still need a careful and experienced education.

On the question of colour, the best thing to do is to go for what you like but be prepared to be flexible. I have yet to hear circumstantial evidence that black labradors really are better workers than yellow or that liver and white spaniels are more trainable than black and white spaniels. It is work that counts and colour must be of secondary importance. My only reason for choosing a yellow labrador not a black from a litter was because there are a lot of blacks working locally on our shoots and I thought that I would be able to watch the pup more easily. If you choose a yellow labrador puppy which looks almost white at eight weeks old, you can be fairly sure that it will darken considerably within a year, they almost all do. With spaniels, I like a white end to the tail flag and a good deal of white on the body, but I am short-sighted and find light colours easier to see in undergrowth. There are a few good chocolate labradors about but not enough for me to recommend an amateur to look specifically for one.

Whether to choose a dog or a bitch will depend on several circumstances and, to a certain extent, personal preference. If there are already dogs in the family of one sex, then you must choose that one. Unless all the bitches are spayed it is foolish to mix them because it will precipitate worry and frustration for yourself and the dogs. I think it really fair to say that a bitch is marginally easier to train than a dog and inclined to be less headstrong. I hope that your puppy will not get the opportunity to wander but given the circumstances a dog will be more likely to do so. Some dogs are tiresome with bitches in the shooting field, and a few owners do bring out bitches which should still be in purdah and then your dog will be distracted from his work. I have seen the best dogs lose concentration and need putting on a lead so I settled for bitches years ago. Although some breeders and trainers frown at the practice I think it is sensible for the novice who does not wish to breed to have the bitch spayed at eighteen months old. The operation has now been perfected to such a degree that the bitch should suffer no more than a few days discomfort. We live in a village and for several weeks in the year we would suffer inconvenience from visiting dogs if my bitches came on heat. Having them spayed is a weight off my mind and, indeed, theirs too, because bitches can be distracted by sex and romantic urges as well as dogs. A spayed bitch need not get fat, none of mine have. They are hard and lean and thanks to the operation they never miss a day in the shooting field.

Naturally if you are undecided about breeding and perhaps have a family line that you wish to carry on then leave the bitch alone, because once spayed she can never be bred from. The pro's and con's of breeding from the family gundog will be discussed in a later chapter. Dogs can now be castrated without detriment to character, but I have no experience of whether this is wise for a gundog or whether there is risk of impairing the animal's natural style and drive for work.

Avoid a show strain and always buy a working puppy in the country or at least from a breeder or family whom you know for certain to be involved in shooting work on a regular basis. Get in your mind's eye the right type to suit you; if it is to be a labrador then look for a wide head, a short otter-type tail and strong legs on a broad chest without heftiness. Go for a middle-size, busy-looking spaniel with intelligent eyes and strong legs set on a good front. Spaniels which resemble miniature greyhounds in any way should be avoided. Of course when you choose the puppy you will not be able to recognise all these virtues but you must see at least one, and preferably both, the parents. I like what we term in this part of the country a 'keeper's spaniel', and always go for the small, lithe tough little canines which are bred for work on the grouse moors. Advertisements in local papers or in such journals as *The Field*, *Shooting Times* and *Shooting News* may yield a good young dog, but I do regard them as a second resort, not to be confused with a last resort. Lots of these dogs will be excellent but if they were all as good as cracked up to be, why haven't they already been sold to local buyers? There may genuinely be a glut on the market in their locality, it happens at certain times of the year to the best breeders and some may genuinely feel they want to attract a wider market for their goods. All the same, I do advise the novice to look in his or her own neighbourhood. If it is a shooting area, and we hope it will be, then good puppies will be there. Gamekeepers are usually friendly men provided you chat to them when they are off duty. Get some local information as to who has a good strain and might be likely to have a puppy of the type and breed to suit you. Having found a kennel, if the trainer or gamekeeper is not prepared to go out of his way to show you the sire or dam, or both if possible, and to demonstrate his dogs working abilities under natural conditions, then go elsewhere. There are plenty of good men and women who know how important this is and will go to a lot of trouble to be sure the puppy is going to suit the owner. If you are buying a trained dog you will need at the very least, three lessons with the breeder/trainer in how to handle it. Fix this up as a certainty before committing yourself.

Look carefully at the puppy's mouth and avoid an undershot jaw. Too many hard mouthed dogs have a tendency to be undershot and it cannot be a coincidence. Gun shyness is not now so common as it used to be, largely due to improved and enlightened training methods and gadgets like dummy launchers which simulate gunfire. Many puppies described as gun shy are often just gun nervous. If you buy an adult trained dog this problem will not arise and with a puppy from a good working strain it is unlikely to be a problem. Whining is the third incurable and when a dog really starts making a noise it is a real curse and I will discuss the problem in another chapter. Spaniels are more likely to develop the habit than labradors or one of the H.P.R. breeds.

A keeper friend of mine with a very good strain of working spaniels tells me that he likes to sit among his pups and let them play in the grass at his feet. He throws his cap for them to fetch and learns a lot about their characters by watching them. When I suggested that by getting them to fetch up his cap he was picking out the likely good retrievers, he remonstrated at once. 'They are all good retrievers,' he assured me. 'Not one of them will not do it quite naturally . . .' This goes for all puppies from parents of proven working ability so choose the pup which appeals to you in a litter, because she is as likely to have a similar aptitude for work as her siblings. A puppy which appears rather nervous or difficult must not be discarded automatically. With patience and time she could turn out a first rate worker and be easier to handle than her bold brothers and sisters. However, it is wise to avoid a misery which scuttles off to hide as soon as the kennel door is opened.

A puppy aged eight to ten weeks from any good shooting strain is likely to cost eighty to one hundred pounds. It will then need inoculations and some basic equipment so that will be another fifty pounds, possibly more. A large poof costs fifteen pounds, a basket more and a kennel runs into the hundreds. More may need to be spent on lessons from a trainer, or a session at a dog training course like those now admirably run by the Game Conservancy and the British Association for Shooting and Conservation. If you choose to have your bitch spayed, that will be another forty-five pounds.

A fully trained dog of eighteen months to two years can cost anything between four hundred and one thousand pounds. It is expensive, but you could spend nearly as much on bringing on a

A good puppy will be a natural retriever

puppy yourself if you need training help and I think for a first dog it could be worth the initial expense. If you do not offer an efficient working image when you start out, then not many landowners or keepers are likely to ask you to help them. It will be marginally less expensive if you buy the puppy at eight weeks old and take it home for six months and then send it back to the kennel for three or four months training. If it is his own breeding, at least the trainer will not tell you it is a no-hoper after a few weeks, but will do his best to make a good job of the dog.

Whichever training procedure you decide to adopt, it is going to cost money. Quality counts and does not come cheap. I can assure you that you will not regret one penny of your outlay when your pride and joy retrieves a difficult runner to hand.

CHAPTER FOUR

Routine and Discipline in the Home Environment

Good gundogs in the hands of professionals are found throughout their lives in one of several situations. In their kennels, out under control with their handler in the shooting field or indoors lying at their owner's feet. There is no lack of exercise, discipline or love in this way of life.

We read much about manners and training in the course of the dog's work in the field, but what of the day to day routine? Many men cannot undertake responsibility for a dog five days in the week and it is often left to the housewife to be supervisor. Lucky the woman whose husband is a farmer because he will be responsible for exercising his own protégé, although judging by the gundogs I have seen hunting the hedgerows and feathering about on the stubble beside farming owners, I am doubtful whether I should allow my gundogs to accompany a farmer around his fields every morning. More harm can be done to an impressionable young dog hanging around master, whose attention must necessarily be engaged elsewhere, than by leaving him in the company of the family in the garden. Young children need not necessarily spoil a gundog for his work in the field. This is a convenient excuse for the man whose own shortcomings have reduced a biddable animal to an unresponsive one. Naturally, if children are allowed to use the words of command about the house which the dog has learnt in the field, or to throw balls for him to retrieve, then damage will be done. But no mother worth her salt who cares a rap for the dog's performance in the field need allow them to do this. Commonsense should dictate a sensible code of behaviour, and, in so many ways, the training of intelligent young dogs is not unlike the training of young children.

When a gundog is given, or can take, its liberty, then problems will inevitably arise and the following season's work in the shooting field will show a marked deterioration in the standard of the animal's work. The essence of gundog training is that, faced with the temptation of moving game, the dog will stop. I do not mean hesitate, or pause, before feathering on, but a definite stop. Once a gundog gets into the habit of chasing, all chance of efficient control is lost. Of course obedience is the quintessense of training and I shall stress this repeatedly, but it will be of little use in the long term once the dog has learnt the joys of self-hunting. An unsupervised dog can slip off, at first only for a short maraud and then, realising that no one is interested in his whereabouts, for a longer one. Roaming hedgerows and fields alone will inevitably lead to the dog discovering the joys of self-hunting and that will be the end of your efficient shooting companion.

With all habits, prevention is better than cure. A gundog must either be confined to its living quarters or out under control of its handler, or someone prepared to be responsible for him all the time that he is out. This may seem to be a loss of liberty, but a little thought will indicate its necessity. A gundog is a working dog and he will not remain efficient if he is not treated like one. The modern gundog has been bred with working capabilities of paramount importance. Most of them are not restful, domesticated creatures content to snooze peacefully by the baby's pram on the lawn. It is a salient fact that gamekeepers always house their dogs outside. It is rare for a keeper's wife to have the working dogs in her home and, having owned gundogs myself, I can appreciate why.

Working dogs are happier and healthier if they sleep in good outside accommodation. Whether they stay there all day as well as all night is a matter for individual arrangement. My own gundogs do come into the house, when it is convenient during the day, but they sleep outside and can be confined outside when we do not want to have them underfoot. We feel that they get the best of both worlds. They regard their kennel as a safe haven which they know is their own and they are content to be left there if I am busy. They also love the warm kitchen. For security reasons I do often leave them in the house when I am out. So if outside accommodation can be arranged, the novice's new gundog should sleep outside. It will save wear and tear on carpets, after all every dog needs letting out in the mornings and it is often wet underfoot. I find a good routine is to let them out of the kennel for a run before breakfast and then confinement again for an hour or two while household chores are done and their paws and coats

To prevent roaming, the dog can be confined to a kennel

dry off. They have individual poofs and baskets in the kitchen alongside the house dogs furniture.

In these days of enlightment and wide advertising it would seem superfluous to discuss kennel arrangements and much will depend upon existing facilities, but a surprising number of dog owners appear not to have the least idea of a dog's needs in this respect. A dark, damp shed will not do. Quite apart from humanity, if the dog is to be kennelled, then everything possible should be done to preserve health and contentment. Weatherproof, draughtless and roomy kennels can now be easily obtained. If the dog is always to be confined outside then a concrete run will be needed and this must have provision for rapid disposal of surplus water. Kennel manufacturers offer every conceivable size and shape of kennel and at all prices. Information is readily obtainable from manufacturers' catalogues. It is usually possible to run an electric cable from the house and if heating is to be provided, and electricity is obtainable, it is the healthiest and safest method of warming a kennel. In fact, our kennel is not heated. The dogs have a deep bed of old hay, which I prefer to straw and they keep very cosy. Palatial kennels will be beyond the purse of many owners who should utilize a shed or put one up from the D.I.Y. shop. Doors and windows should preferably face south or south westerly so that cold winds from east and north do not penetrate the interior. The floor must be raised from the ground with an outside awning as protection against hot sun and driving rain, and a low bar fixed across the bottom of the door to prevent bedding going astray. The interior dimensions must be sufficiently high and wide to permit the dog to stand up or stretch comfortably. The kennel or shed must not be built in a hollow where water can collect or damp become a problem. Paths and yards which are not hard-surfaced can quickly become wet and muddy underfoot. It is worth the expense of concreting a path and a small access area.

Dogs which spend time in the house must be disciplined and the drill starts as soon as the puppy arrives. It is tiresome when visitors call if the dogs make a nuisance of themselves roaming round everyone's ankles. Jumping up on strangers and children must be stopped at once and young labradors and golden retrievers are especially inclined to demonstrate affection in this way. Young visiting children can be frightened by this habit and object noisily, and the resultant commotion is bewildering for a young dog, so teach her early to keep all four feet on the ground, however exuberant she may be feeling. If she does not respond to being pushed firmly down, then step on her hind feet as she places her forefeet endearingly on your chest and she will soon find it uncomfortable to continue the habit. Send the dog to its basket when it is inconvenient to have her underfoot and, what is more important, see that she stays there. If you persist in sending her back to her corner and keep your eye on her so that she is aware of vigilance then she will get the message.

What is the etiquette on a walk with a gundog, how much freedom can she enjoy and where does one draw the line? Alas, so many good young dogs are spoilt by wild walks. But it really is almost impossible for a parent to take young children for a walk over the fields, chatting them up, not to speak of probably picking them up bodily, meanwhile keeping an eye on the exuberant young dog which is having a glorious time in the nearest hedgerow. Those of our colleagues who are not domiciled in the country, so that every walk is a medley of glorious gamey smells, are actually more fortunate and more likely to preserve their dog's education. Beaches and public parks are more restful, because here we can allow the dog freedom without the uneasy feeling that she might put up a hare and chase it into the next parish, to the detriment of all those early days shooting when so much trouble was taken to stop just this sort of situation arising. So avoid the temptations offered by game on walks when it is not possible to give adequate supervision to the dog. Boring though the route may become, choose a walk where there are no temptations and allow the dog reasonable freedom. She must be allowed to gallop freely for a while when she is young. I try to keep one eye on the dogs all the time and only call them in when they are getting out of gun range. Summer months are easier; we can be out pottering in the garden and doing outside chores like hanging up washing and gardening. This gives the dog interest and exercise and a daily walk is not such a necessity.

The modern estate car is so designed that gundog owners have never had it so easy. Dirty paws on upholstery are an abomination but it really is a struggle to teach strong-minded canines that their place is on the floor of the vehicle and not on the seats. So we have the dog guard or barrier and they are worth every penny of the investment. Teach the dog to wait before getting in or out of a vehicle. It is infuriating to have dirty dogs crowding unbidden into the estate vehicles before the guns. Some drives are near roads and it is very dangerous if a dog leaps out haphazardly as soon as the door of the vehicle is opened. Car drill must always be strictly enforced. When the dog is let out of the vehicle its predilection is to jump up and run around excitedly. Make her sit quietly in the car while you get your coat on and bits and pieces gathered together. A moment of control in what is an exciting situation. Only then may she jump out and run free for a few minutes to let off steam and check what is going on.

Car sickness is something which will almost certainly pass, but can cause temporary inconvenience and worry. Pills from the vet help and short car rides will have to be arranged. The young labrador that I have at present was dreadfully sick in the car as a puppy but was completely cured by the time she was eight months old.

In this age of convenience foods, the fact that the dog is a carnivore, or meat-eating animal, is sometimes lost sight of and a preponderance of proprietory brands of food in the dogs' bowls must get rather boring. I have to admit, however, that the dogs look very well on complete foods and breeders and trainers must use them. A high or a low protein diet can be fed. An interesting study can be made of the bewildering variety of tinned products on offer. If you buy tinned, frozen or dried meat it pays to be discriminating. Many are good and do contain a reasonable quantity of meat but there are a few which do not match up to their showy labels and descriptions and carry a

Car discipline must be started at an early age

preponderance of cereal. Check with a good trainer or breeder in the neighbourhood whose dogs look fit and well and be guided by his experience and advice. He may have an agency for a good brand and be able to supply you regularly.

My dogs enjoy a variety of foods, are always lean and fit and live to a ripe old age. I buy rabbits from a local keeper's son. There are hundreds in the countryside around here, so the landowner does not mind the boy shooting them and he gets fifty pence a couple, paunched but not skinned. I cook them and the dogs love them but I do get tired of picking the meat off those tiny bones. A friend tells me that a pressure cooker will reduce the bones to jelly so that would be helpful, and nutritious for the dogs. We get a fair amount of venison coming into the house and I feed cooked lights, hearts, scrap and rib meat and torn livers. The freezer is a boon for storing these bits raw and I have never owned a dog which did not love venison. It is surprising how quickly I can get new dogs onto this meat with no ill effects on their tummies. Surplus vegetables from the garden are good for variety and a friend told me that her labrador's arthritis was greatly eased by feeding him raw cabbage.

Staying with friends or in hotels it is not wise to accept proffered fare for the dogs, much safer to take your own. Dogs' tummies can react to a change of diet and bedroom carpets will suffer.

Labradors are greedy and tend to run to fat so never feed titbits. This maxim holds good for all breeds. Up to four months old a puppy needs three meals a day, two meals up to six or seven months, and thereafter only one. Our dogs are fed about five o'clock and this fits in well with a shooting day.

CHAPTER FIVE

Training Days for Gundogs

The Game Conservancy and the British Association for Shooting and Conservation arrange Training days in different areas of the country. Having seen the poor standard of amateur dog work prevalent today, these organisations felt that there might be a need for help and enthusiasts have supported them in large numbers. Both courses are concerned with practical work in the field, not with working tests or trial work.

Sixty of us gathered at ten o'clock on a late summer morning in the old walled garden of a stately home for a Game Conservancy Dog Day being held in Yorkshire. We had been told to leave our own dogs at home, there was to be no time for individual lessons. In the lecture hall, we were introduced to our speaker/demonstrators – in this case, a spaniel man as well as a retriever man. The first session took us through choosing the breed to suit different needs and individuals, sex and age. This led to housing, feeding and understanding the animal's personality, weaknesses and strengths. We were told how to use the voice, the hands and to build up good eye contact with the dog. We must learn to try and think like a dog and to see things as he, or she, would. Easier for some than others, but this was clearly considered of importance. This was followed by a demonstration in the walled garden with two young labradors being given early lessons in sitting, staying, walking to heel and getting accustomed to gunfire and dummy work. The spaniel man then showed us what could be done with two springers, both full of potential. They worked enthusiastically, full of drive but how easily they would spoil in the wrong hands. Interesting to see how different the work is for labradors and spaniels being demonstrated by professionals. As the dogs worked, the trainers explained what they were trying to achieve and, as these were young dogs, not everything went exactly as planned.

Spectators watching a dog training display. Newby, Yorkshire 1986

John Halstead is one of the Game Conservancy Training Day Instructors

Inside again, the pro's and con's of who should train the shooting dog were discussed, whether it was to be the amateur himself or a professional trainer; also how bolting rabbits, dummy launchers and other accessories can be used or, in some cases, misused. First introduction to gunfire, water and natural obstacles. We were encouraged to ask questions and to take part in discussion. Our speakers stressed that the course was only a guide and that none of us must be under the misapprehension that they were suggesting instant training.

During the afternoon, we watched advanced training with an introduction to cold game and to freshly shot game. Natural conditions were used, with the dogs working thick cover and retrieving from water. The day ended with tea and plenty of opportunity to talk to the two speakers. This was worthwhile and as a preliminary to owning a dog it was useful, but it was clear that once a dog was spoilt for work there was no magic cure to be found by going to a Dog Day and hoping to find a solution to the problem. It would be advisable for the novice to go to one of these demonstration days run by the Game Conservancy either in the initial stages of his dog's schooling or, preferably, before buying a dog.

Two weeks later, I enrolled on a B.A.S.C. Gundog Training day course being held at a county Agricultural College. On these one-day courses delegates are encouraged to bring their own dogs, although this is not necessary. This turned out to be quite different from the Game Conservancy's course because we had to do much of the work ourselves. I took my young labrador and joined eighteen other amateur handlers exercising their dogs in the College car park before meeting our instructor, the B.A.S.C. Honorary Gundog Advisor himself who had travelled up from the south to be with us. We must have looked a daunting prospect to be sorted out, a motley collection of young gundogs of varying breeds, ages, sexes and sizes.

'Twenty candidates is the maximum that I can help in one day,' our instructor told us. 'I think audience participation is important. I can't produce a trained gundog in one day but I aim to show the handler, how, by following the right sequence of proven methods, it is within his capabilities to train his own dog.'

We started with basic obedience, heel work, sit and stay and continued to more advanced training and steadiness to shot. The dogs demonstrated varying degrees of enthusiasm and inattention and the handlers did their best to keep their pupils minds on the job. For most of us this was not difficult, anyone with a dog over a year old had an

Instruction on a Game Conservancy Training Day

eager participant on the end of the lead, some of the juveniles were not so keen. Within the first hour our trainer had sized up his class, he knew the dogs and was able to show us where we were going wrong and how to put things straight again. One lad had his dog's choke chain on upside down. It was fascinating to watch, and to learn, from other peoples' problems and to see how the trainer handled individual cases. Most of the dogs showed promise and by lunchtime we had all relaxed and were enjoying the lessons. It is good discipline to watch others working their dogs and for our own to learn that not every retrieve was to be for them. There was plenty of time for questions and discussion. Periodically, we rested the dogs and went back into the lecture hall to discuss housing, feeding, general training, and choosing accessories like whistles, leads and dog beds.

Lunch was a relaxed affair with our trainer discussing dog work with us whilst we ate our sandwiches. There were some very fine green canvas dummies on the sales table but we were shown how to make our own, practical dummies made out of hessian, just the right size and weight for a young dog. Moreover, I now know how to make another when the one I made on this course gets floppy with use.

Later live accessories were produced. It is impressive to see the paraphenalia which B.A.S.C. provide. Pigeons in a basket gave an introduction to game, later they were released and persuaded to fly, at the gun's report, whilst we 'hupped' our dogs. Rabbit skins attached to elastic shot past under our dogs' noses as we did a simulated walk-up and pigeons ejected from traps, set in the long grass. We could not have asked for better training under natural conditions. Our canine pupils were pop-eyed, in varying degrees of steadiness. Dummies were thrown out, handlers giving hand signals under direction, learning how to cope with each step of their dog's education. By the end of the day we were nearly as exhaused as our trainer must have been, but both we, and our dogs, had enjoyed a very worthwhile exercise.

So the training courses offered by the Game Conservancy and B.A.S.C. are both valuable, but different in approach. The former offer more of a demonstration to amateur handlers and the latter welcome amateur's own dogs and guide them through various stages of training. As a result of attending one of these Training Days, the novice must benefit considerably. It is also enjoyable and helpful to meet new friends with mutual interests. Do think seriously about going along to the nearest one being held in your part of the country. Which training day you choose is a matter for personal preference. The different approach does not conflict so why not follow my example and try both.

CHAPTER SIX

Basic Canine Psychology

Whether the reader has decided to have his dog trained by a professional or is going to train it himself, he is going to have a young dog to humanise and educate on his own premises. A routine and a code of manners for the animal will have to be worked out. Discipline and obedience is the name of the game.

Many years ago, a wise friend of mine who had had a succession of useful canine shooting companions, told me never to give my dog an order which I was not certain of being able to enforce. This is very good advice. I took heed of this counsel and it is one of the prime reasons why my dogs are obedient. When someone comes to the garden gate and the dogs hurry across to see who is coming, it is foolish to call a young dog in when the chances of her obeying instantly are slim. If the pup is going to integrate in family life and join in walks with the house dogs, it is neither possible or necessary for your shooting companion to be always at heel or to come instantly to recall if she is indulging in some gambolling games with the other dogs in the paddock or yard. If every outing is a training one, she will never learn about the good things in life, the woods and the fields and the fun of running free. The secret is to avoid putting temptation in the way by never allowing the dog to be out of your sight. Snuffling down a hedgerow on the heady scent of a rabbit, the dog is unlikely to respond enthusiastically to a command. The first time of asking she may do so reluctantly, the next time with even less enthusiasm and within weeks she will have become slack to commands and the rot will have set in. So never go where there is game unless you are on a training walk. Dogs are not as intelligent as humans and they live entirely for the moment. Your dog will not hold it against you if the walk is boring because she is not mentally comparing it with where she might be. So you have the upper hand at the start. Stick to a few basic rules and the dog will become your servant.

Gundogs can easily be led astray by family dogs – terriers are born ringleaders

When I bought my first springer spaniel, trained, but, as the wise keeper who sold her to me remarked, 'Ready to spoil . . .' I realised then that I must make certain rules and we would stick rigidly to them. I have done this with success and I do commend the novice owner to do likewise. The use of the whistle, and the words of command which I learnt during my lessons on the moor with this man, I decided to keep strictly for training walks only. My whistle and my 'shooting voice' I use for the short daily training lessons and for work in the shooting field. This plan has worked well and the dogs know at once when it is business and respond by being sharply obedient. If the reader's dog is to be a house dog and will integrate with family life, I do commend this plan, otherwise, even with the best intentions, rules get slack and, inevitably, training suffers.

We have all seen men and women telling their dogs to 'sit' whilst talking to friends. The dog obeys and remains momentarily in situ, but within a very short time he has risen from his haunches and moved away. Engaged in conversation, his owner permits this lapse or does not notice it. If the order is not going to be strictly enforced then it is better not to give it at all. Dogs are not fools and will quickly realise if master is not really concerned whether they sit

Avoid temptation and never allow a gundog to maraud alone

correctly or not. If you do not want the dog to wander out of the garden gate or to investigate a smell in the hedgerow whilst you are engaged in conversation, then call the dog in to your proximity but do not ask her to sit unless you are going to see that she does so. Exactly the same applies to walking to heel. Pointless to nag 'heel' at the dog repeatedly and fail to see that she does stay correctly beside you. No wonder that as a result dogs get slack and fail to respond immediately when orders are given in the shooting field. So keep those important words of command to be used on the field strictly for battle conditions.

Some women are better at disciplining gundogs than their husbands and it may well be because men find it difficult to concentrate on more than one thing at a time. Women have a gift of being able to watch several things going on at the same time whilst engaged in doing something else. Gundogs should not be left unsupervised while their owners enjoy their garden. If I am hanging up the washing or planting my wall flowers, I am still keeping an eye on where the dogs are. No one gets a chance to slip away to investigate a hedgerow. If they did, it would be the end of my efficient shooting companions. However, if my husband is planting the potatoes or washing his car he finds it impossible to watch the dogs as well. On the credit side it must be said, however, he makes a much better job of what he is doing than I do because with my butterfly mind I am trying to do too many things at once. All the same, the dogs don't suffer and I make sure that I know what they are up to. If they are not under my eye, I put them in the kennel. There is no need to fret about this seeming loss of liberty because a little thought will indicate its necessity. Troubles come to gundogs when they are given, or can take, their liberty.

Watch a good dog trainer and notice how he maintains eye contact all the time with his pupil. The dog is alert and responsive, eager to obey. This important eye contact is your substitute for a dog lead. Try not to rely on a lead. Far too many dogs are brought out on shoots attached to their owners at an impressionable age, and when I see them again several years later they are attached to master's waist by a chain.

The idea is to build up a thread between you, a rapport which your pupil will be aware is a personal trust or relationship. Dogs are basically servile creatures, at least most gundog breeds are, and adore being willing servants. So, instead of a lead, use an invisible thread which is the eye and the voice. Once you have established this contact it will suffice if you work at keeping it up and never get slack about the dog's manners and obedience. If I put a lead on, and under certain circumstances I occasionally do, then at once the dog's dependence upon me is broken and she no longer has to answer to me for her actions.

I like to put my dogs on leads when men and dogs are piling into landrovers to take us up to the grouse moor. The same applies at the start of any big shoot, especially with a young dog which does not know the drill. The anticipation and excitment of the moment is confusing for any dog and I like to see that my rule of waiting for an order to jump in and out of a vehicle is strictly adhered to. I have known large boisterous labradors and golden retrievers literally knock my waiting spaniels out of the back of the vehicle using my knickbockered knees as a springboard in their haste to depart. Under these conditions I prefer to keep them attached to me.

Another situation which justifies a lead is in the beating line when we approach a big flush of pheasants. Very often at the end of a covert birds are hunched in petrified gaggles, hiding in any available undergrowth. Your dog may not run in and cause a flurry, but a young dog, especially a spaniel may 'peg' birds. This means nailing and retrieving crouching pheasants. Some of the best dogs can do it and should be forgiven but obviously the habit is undesirable. So on big days, when birds are hopping and crouching and dipping in the brambles or along the last ditch at the end of the covert, then it is policy to put on a lead.

The essence of handling your gundog is to think out a sensible routine of work and play and to stick to it. When I got my first dog, I had three school age children and a toddler, but we got on well and she introduced me to several estates where we have been able to make ourselves useful and have had a lot of fun doing so. She was trained by an expert and handled by a total amateur. We succeeded because I made these simple rules and stuck by them.

CHAPTER SEVEN

Early Lessons

For the first four months of the puppy's life do not attempt any training at all. It will be five and a half months before the canine teeth are shed. Family manners should be gradually introduced but the dog must be allowed to grow up and enjoy herself and become accustomed to the routine and the environment where she is going to live. A good puppyhood is important so that when she is at an age for formal training she will be free of inhibitions and bad habits. Never allow the family to try out any commands at all. This must be exclusively your job or the trainer's. I like to take a puppy about in my car from four months old onwards, to train her to walk on a lead and to allow her to meet groups of people. This widens the puppy's experience without pressurising and makes the transition to a training schedule (particularly if the dog is going into kennels for this period) less stressful.

A surprising number of puppies have travelling problems and are bad passengers at an early age. A mile or two in the car and they throw up. Uncomfortable for the dog and messy and inconvenient for the owner. Modern vehicles are smoother and more soporific than the early models that my father conveyed his dogs around in, and I never remember any problems with his dogs. Many distraught puppy owners have asked me about this problem and imagine that their shooting companion is going to be unable to travel beyond a radius of five miles from the kennel. Nine cases out of ten clear up within a year. Take the puppy for short runs, make her sit on the floor, or in the back if it is an estate car, and the problem will clear up within months. If it does not do so by the time she is twelve months old, then get some pills from the vet. Basically, this is a nervous problem. Once the young dog is relaxed and accepts the car journey as normal routine she will stop panting, dribbling or being sick.

It is important to allow the pup to meet people. Every shoot assembly is the preliminary to a day's work and this will mean strangers talking in loud voices and probably several excited dogs. A nervous dog could find this off-putting if she has never been in a crowd. Put a lead on the pup and take her around with you to a few family and country events.

You will need a light rope lead to slip over the dog's neck during training. I like the quick release lead to carry in my pocket out shooting. You will have to decide whether you intend to use a whistle or to rely upon the voice and a restraining 'sss-t'. The latter is a useful noise which has the effect of conveying correction to dogs with scarcely any training preliminary. Useful for a dog which edges forward from her position at heel or feathers after scent in the grass instead of remaining glued to your side. If you have a quiet voice which nevertheless commands respect (and many of the best trainers have) then you may be able to get away without a whistle, which will probably be much more satisfactory, because there are usually several other people blasting away in the shooting field, which must be confusing for the dogs. However, there are times when the dog is out of reasonable ear shot of the voice and needs help or a pause for re-direction and I have found a stag horn whistle an essential accessory. Two blasts for re-call, one long one for stop and a short sharp one to indicate a turn is our whistle vocabulary. If your puppy is to be trained for you, leave it to the trainer to decide the type of whistle, and what signals he will train your dog to, and ask to buy the whistle from him when you collect your trained dog. Possibly he may ask you to provide a whistle, this is a matter for negotiation. There are 'silent' whistles on the market which are supposed to be indistinguishable to a human ear, but command obedience from a canine. The only time I have seen them used, the dogs apparently could not hear them either. Anyone with a loud or sharp voice must sometimes use a whistle because nothing is worse on a shoot than a human voice. No keeper wants his birds running like stags into the next parish because of a noisy gun, or picker-up.

Canvas dummies designed to fit comfortably into a dog's mouth are readily on sale and you will need a dummy even if your dog is going away to be trained. I make my own by sewing up two rabbit skins stuffed with old stockings. Go on a B.A.S.C. Dog Training day course and learn to make a hessian one. To accustom a puppy to retrieve birds, I tie pheasant feathers on the dummy and the pup is always very proud of carrying the plumage. However, I have never had a sticky retriever and I am sure this is because I have taken great care to choose puppies from genuine working blood lines, with both parents being proven retrievers. Check the dummy regularly if it is home-made to be sure that stuffing, stitches, feathers or fur are not coming astray. The dummy should be a firm object, not a floppy one. I do not like putting hard cheese or food of any kind in a dummy because a greedy puppy might be tempted to sniff or crunch or maul it and all of these habits are undesirable.

Decide on a working vocabulary and keep it for work so that the dog knows that you mean business and will brook no disobedience. With minor variation, I suggest the following:

Hup, or Sit. (Always associated in early training with a raised hand.)
Heel.
Wait, or Stay.
Hi-lost.
Over.
Come-in. (Associated in early training with patting my knee and blowing re-call on the whistle.)
Sss-t.
No.

This is my vocabulary and, apart from 'No', 'Sit', 'Heel' and 'Over', I only use words during training sessions or whilst we are on the shoot. You could use Hup to put the dog down and also Sit to get her to sit and relax. My Hup seems to have been adequate to sit my dogs but I have a labrador now which strongly resisted sitting during training, prefering to crouch and as she is a very nervous dog I have accepted this. At nearly three years old she has begun to sit of her own accord and I now use Sit as a command for her and she has learnt to obey either word. So you may have to adapt the vocabulary to suit your individual but try to keep it simple and never let the children or friends give your dog orders otherwise slackness, instead of instant compliance will result. Heel is self-explanatory. No, is really a domestic word and generally only used in puppyhood, it is a word which seems to be readily understood. Hopefully, you will not use it much. It is, of course, a corrective term. Wait, is my own invention and I use it to discipline the dogs at gates and fences out shooting. It is bad manners to have gundogs pushing through gates and through fences before the shooting party have gone through. When I have to climb a wall (which we frequently do in this county whilst beating) or I must get over, or through, a wire fence, then I do not want my dogs feathering across the next field whilst I am negotiating a tricky obstacle. A young dog soon learns that she is more agile than a human being. So teach the dogs to wait at every wall, hedge, gate or fence for an order to go on. Only occasionally have I found this to be a slowing-up process when a dog was on a runner, and a hand signal quickly dispels doubts and sends the dog on. I also use the word Wait when loading and unloading the dogs into the car. The only one which will not obey is our dachsund who sets a bad example to the other dogs.

Hi-lost is the order the dogs all love and none hesitate over obeying that one. Some trainers differentiate between whether the bird is a marked one or not, but I have not found this necessary and I do try to make my vocabulary as simple as possible. Over, is used for jumping walls, fences or wide streams.

At the beginning of training, it is best to start by calling the pup in rather than whistling, so I use Come-in and lead on to the whistle, again, in conjunction with a hand signal which is often useful later on when silence is golden in the shooting field. I can frequently just tap my knee to bring a dog readily in to heel. Sss-t is an invaluable noise and less distracting for fellow guns, pickers-up or beaters as well as being very effective as a signal to the dog that although I may appear to be engaged in conversation, nevertheless my beady eye is still on my responsibilities. There are times when it is impolite not to socialise although I do try and keep away from conversationalists in the shooting field when I have a young dog out. It is rude and off-putting to be continually grumbling at a dog, so Sss-t is useful here.

Seventy yards behind the guns at your picking-up stand or struggling through brambles or waist high bracken in the beating line, then there is nothing to stop you having a chat with the dogs, calling them any names you like. Encouraging the young ones is particularly important. But this must all be done in low tones so that no one else on the field can be distracted. Otherwise, keep orders to a minimum to avoid confusion and do not issue any words of command unless you are in a position to see that they will be obeyed.

On every shooting day, we see adult gundogs being lifted over fences, coaxed between wires and heaved over stiles. They are agile enough when it comes to getting over or through anything in pursuit of a runner. But some seem to be unwilling to negotiate obstacles when not on a hot scent and the whole shooting party is held up whilst

Teach the dog to wait at every gate for an order to come on

Tap your knee when whistling for a dog to come in

a dog is persuaded to use his initiative. Every puppy should be taken on interesting walks where he will meet natural obstacles. If at all possible, leave the young dog to work out her own salvation unless the problem is taut barbed wire – an unpleasant hazard now only too common. The youngster will quickly understand that she is expected to work out a route for herself. You can do a lot to teach her at an impressionable age but do not start helping her unless it is strictly necessary. Most dogs love jumping; start small and avoid walls and strong timber until legs get stronger. A good clean jumper is an asset and if she has been taught to Wait for a signal to go on, this gives you an opportunity to prevent jumping or squeezing over or through barbed wire. Every shooting season we see dogs with torn feet and undercarriages. I teach my dogs never to try and jump a cattle grid, but immediately to look for a way round as soon as they are permitted to come on.

Introduce the puppy to cattle, sheep, poultry and tractors so that these will not be new phenomena when the dog goes on to the shooting field.

A good clean jumper is a great asset

CHAPTER EIGHT

Professional Training

The puppy that goes to a professional to be trained to the gun will leave home at approximately eight months, depending upon when the trainer considers her ready. This will, of course, have been already booked and terms agreed for training and kennel fee. Gamekeepers are not, necessarily, the best people to train gundogs; they are busy people and not all have biddable dogs themselves. Personal recommendation is preferable to answering an advertisement. Take time and trouble over finding the right man or woman for the job, it may not be necessary to travel many miles, there could be a good trainer in your neighbourhood.

Visit the trainer and see his dogs and his premises. Some of us are fortunate enough to have a paddock and access to land where the dogs can run, but, although desirable, this is not essential for a trainer. The best man I know in our neighbourhood takes his young dogs to the local park for training in his van. His garden is so small he could not possibly allow them to run in it. Owners with house dogs do feel that kennels must necessarily be restrictive and inhibiting for their dogs, but this is not necessarily so, and it is surprising how little most dogs do mind confinement, particularly in company. If the puppy is going to have one or two daily training sessions, then the confinement of a kennel can be beneficial because training can be physically and mentally exhausting.

Notice how the dogs greet their trainer, whether dirty feeding bowls are left in their kennels or pens and if the runs and exercise yard have been washed out regularly. I remember one trainer getting a black mark because the poor man had had two dogs stolen from his small exercise yard during the last twelve months. The encircling wall was low enough to be climbed and adjoined common land. The man lost many potential customers because of these thefts.

Responsible trainers only take a few dogs for training at a time so it will be necessary to make early enquiries and to book ahead. The best trainer I know likes to take a puppy at eight to ten months old, depending upon how mature the dog is and to give a three month training period. During this time he expects the dog to achieve a reasonably high standard of handlability (whistle and hand signals) without actually shooting over the dog. He then recommends the owner taking the dog home for about six weeks to asses her, with the idea of the owner consolidating upon this preliminary training. After this, he takes the dog back for introduction to live game (fur and feather) and, hopefully, the end result is a fully trained dog accustomed to picking freshly shot game (but needing more experience) and ready to be taken out in company and used for picking-up/shooting over. The trainer makes a condition that the owner accompanies him on at least three occasions during training so that his commands and training methods are fully understood.

'This programme does help the dog's owner to get involved,' he explained. 'It also seems to help the transition from one handler to another.' The problem is that this may be impractical unless the trainer lives reasonably near the owner, but could be an area for negotiation. Different trainers have different training schedules, but the above scheme has proved successful for several local guns in this county. One problem is that when the puppy has returned to its family home for the six week break in the middle of training, some owners think that they can finish off training themselves and decide not to send the dog back for the second session.

'This is a pity for me,' the trainer said. 'Because in too many cases the owner does not, or cannot, finish the job satisfactorily. But I get the blame and my reputation suffers.'

Too many amateurs buy well trained dogs and do not know how to handle them. It is essential, therefore, whether buying an adult trained gundog or sending a puppy away to be trained, that the owner goes along for several lessons in how to handle the dog. Potentially excellent dogs can be quickly ruined because their owners do not take this rule seriously enough. 'Such a pity that I was too busy to go along . . .' remarked one man last season. 'But I fixed up for two of the children to watch a training session and they'll keep me right!' Needless to say, the promising springer spaniel in question was hopelessly confused after half a dozen days work in the shooting field with his new master and ruined by the end of his first season. Anyone who is too busy to learn how to handle the new recruit is being unfair to dog and trainer and wasting money.

When a friend of mine went to collect, a young dog which was being trained and which had spent the first seven months of his life with her family, the trainer insisted that she stay hidden while he gave a demonstration of what the dog could do. Only then did he allow my friend to show herself. It must be unsettling to be visited by ghosts from the past when you are supposed to be concentrating. After several more visits my friend was encouraged to stand with the trainer and he suggested that she give the commands and signals which by this time she had fully learned. This man is a particularly thoughtful trainer and, needless to say, now a very successful one.

An increasing number of trainers are now reluctant to send trained dogs on approval. This, of course, applies to adult dogs supplied by the trainer and not having been brought in for training as a pup by the owner. It amazes me how many still do let their charges out for a week without any guarantee of a sale. I met an army officer only last season who had a strong black labrador dog on a week's approval. He picked up behind the guns with me and I was impressed by the excellent marking ability which the dog displayed. He was a super retriever and brought in several spectacular runners. The officer could see what a fine dog he had found, but he had no idea how to handle him. By the end of the second day, the dog was running-in with gusto, unable to believe his luck in being given so many lovely pheasants to bring in. As it turned out, the officer decided to buy the dog. Alas, he is now, a year later, fastened securely to his master's waist by a chain and being so strong he nearly has the wretched man flat on his back every time a bird drops out of the sky. A salutory tale, but, alas, a true one. The trainer did, in this case, achieve a sale but he would be sad to see this dog now. He could just as easily have been handed back as 'unsuitable', after a week breaking every rule he had just learnt.

So, if you decide to buy a trained dog without having had it as a puppy then be certain to take the trouble to become well acquainted with the animal and the way that he has been trained. You are unlikely to get a trial and it won't help you much if you do. Moreover, do not be foolish enough to take the dog home one day and expect him to perform like a paragon in the shooting field the next. He may, but he equally may disappoint and the poor fellow can scarcely be blamed. A new environment, a new owner and the excitment of a day's shooting can be too much for many dogs. Give him time to settle and to get to know you.

At present prices, a fully trained gundog could cost anything between six hundred and one thousand pounds. An eight week puppy from a good strain costs eighty to one hundred pounds. Expensive perhaps, but for the fun you will both enjoy together I can assure you it is worth it. I strongly commend a novice to think seriously about buying a trained dog, provided he or she keeps to the above guidelines.

CHAPTER NINE

Early Discipline – Lessons at Home

My advice at the end of the last chapter having been ignored – you have decided to have a try at training your shooting companion yourself. Well, why not, there is no reason why you should not be successful. Training a biddable, born-to-the-gun canine is a straightforward operation and should only require patience, firmness and keeping strictly to a few simple rules. Remember not to push training on too quickly, particularly if the dog is nervous, highly strung or, alternatively, lethargic. Some puppies take longer to mature than others. Buy a good training manual and follow the recommended training schedule.

If possible, training should be two short periods each day but if this is not possible one fifteen minute session will suffice. Go slowly, and only proceed when each lesson is completely understood. Dogs do not forget, nor do they go stale, so a lay-off now and again will not be harmful if you are too busy or if the weather is too hot for lessons. Leave the dog in the kennel or the house and give her a supervised walk or run in the garden. If you have to train in early morning or evening, this is a very good time to do it.

Sitting and walking to heel are the first lessons to teach. The last young dog I had learnt to walk to heel reliably in three weeks and I prefer to give this lesson first. Remember that commands given without accompanying action are so much Greek to the dog. Walking to heel is supposed not to be acceptable to a spaniel but mine have not given trouble over this discipline. Put on a light slip lead, one made from string or binder twine is perfect because the dog gets the impression after a while that she is walking to heel unattached. Slap your left thigh when giving the command and make the dog keep in a comfortable position with her head level with your knee. Give the order 'heel' firmly and sharply giving the impression that you mean business. I like to walk a distance at heel around the garden or the paddock and then allow the dog liberty for a short while before calling her back to heel. Most young dogs readily comply with these lessons if training is commenced at the right age. Take the lead string off after several lessons and use your left hand to tap her head or nose if she edges out of place, and give a sharp order if she attempts to potter. Find a country road and walk her along it at heel so that she becomes used to traffic. I walk through the village with the dogs at heel and they learn to ignore the neighbours who stop and talk, and the tempting little gardens with the open gates. Very good discipline for a young dog.

Introduce 'sit' by pressing the dog down on her haunches and keeping her there until she relaxes. She should quickly get the idea and if you are beside her it is easy. This exercise becomes more difficult when you are detached from one another. Many trainers recommend making a dog sit before putting its food bowl down but I find this unsatisfactory when there are other house dogs to be fed at the same time. Moreover, occasionally my husband or one of the children feed the dogs, and I cannot expect them to use the commands. The young dog would very likely seize the opportunity to be slack about obeying. Stick to giving the orders yourself, use the sit lesson only during training lessons and insist upon total compliance. My heart always sinks when we visit friends and their gundogs are told to sit momentarily whilst they greet us enthusiastically. Of course they don't sit for more than a few minutes because their owners are otherwise occupied and cannot insist upon compliance.

Using the sit lesson during the training session you can begin to leave her to sit, at first only for seconds and then gradually longer. Always walk back to the dog instead of calling her up because an impetuous dog, especially a spaniel, could begin to anticipate the command to come on. Use the whistle to recall using the two toots signal. When obedience has been instilled, you can graduate to the 'hup' command, introducing the stop whistle as you work. Every young gundog is capable of achieving success if these rudiments are insisted upon because natural gifts and tendencies are being cultivated. The handler simply has to repeat the exercises so that the dog reaches the stage where she reacts, without thinking, to commands in varied circumstances.

When retrieving work is begun with the dummy, I have found it helpful to draw up a programme of exercises to be used on a regular

Walk through the village with the dog at heel

basis once the pup gets the idea of picking the dummy and coming in with it. Novices sometimes complain to me that their puppies have grown tired of the dummy after initial enthusiasm and they feel at a deadlock, wondering what to do to revive interest. This has come about because they have no programme to work to and dog and trainer are finding that what began as an exciting game cannot achieve the status of work without direction. With a shy or reluctant retriever, and I hope the reader will not have one as a first pupil, sometimes an experienced dog can help by showing the puppy what to do. With an uncertain or ponderous return do not stand immobile staring anxiously at the puppy but walk away a few yards calling her name and blowing the recall on the whistle. Make certain that you do not do so before the dummy is in her jaws. I like to turn slightly away when the dog comes in and let her hold it for a moment while I praise her. The dummy is her prize and she loves it. One of the reasons why it is wise not to take the dummy in a hurry is because when you are working several dogs and they chance to arrive back together, each with a bird, they should wait holding their retrieve, while each is taken in turn. A keen dog can get into the bad habit of dumping her bird at your feet and, if your attention is distracted elsewhere, then she may slip off forthwith for another look around. This is most unsatisfactory, because if a runner

Some trainers like the puppy to learn to sit to give up the dummy

Make certain when throwing a dummy which the dog can see, that she sits immediately

is brought in, very likely the poor bird will set off again and you, or your retriever if she is still with you, will have to go ignominiously in pursuit. Bird dropping can become a most undesirable habit so avoid sowing the seeds of this dilemma. Some trainers like a dog to sit up to give up the dummy but this is a refinement which I have not found necessary in the shooting field.

I like to let the puppy run around freely during retrieving lessons so that she does not associate the dummy with work and become bored. What is essential is to make certain that when throwing a dummy which the dog can see, she sits or hups immediately. This is an important drill for the dog must learn that when a bird falls from the air its reaction must be to sit until told to move. We vary the terrain and I blow my stop whistle from time to time and go up and fondle the pup. It is a lesson but it is also fun for both of us. The dog remains alert and responsive, anticipating that the dummy may need fetching in. Never get slack and always insist upon the puppy sitting when she sees the dummy come down. Following your training schedule, make the work more difficult, and more interesting, by throwing the dummy into thick cover or over a ditch. Once I made a foolish mistake and hid it in such a difficult place that neither I, nor the puppy could find it. I had hidden it in long grass under a hedgerow and we still have not found it. I cursed my stupidity, but fortunately the relevant pup was such a keen pupil that she was not discouraged.

A dummy launcher is a useful piece of equipment which enables the trainer to give longer retrieves simulating the real thing, but it is not essential. I do not use one and do not believe that many ladies would wish to do so.

CHAPTER TEN

First Day on the Shoot

The young dog's initiation to retrieving live game is generally in the home environment, as a natural follow-on from the dummy. If you can get work on a grouse moor I have found this the perfect place to introduce a puppy to retrieving feather. Failing that, pigeon shooting makes a good introduction. I have never tried throwing dead birds about the shrubbery or the home paddock where I do my training so this is not necessary unless you cannot get out onto the real thing. It is not a sensible idea to take a young dog out to retrieve live for the first time on a pheasant day where there are likely to be many birds. The most reliable retriever I have ever had spent two weeks dozing beside me whilst I was picking-up on Allenheads grouse moor with spaniels. She was then fourteen months old and experienced with dummies. By the third week she was sitting up taking a keen interest in what her kennel mate was doing and it was then only a matter of days before I marked an easy bird for her. She went off like a rocket and brought it back to hand like a veteran. I kept her beside me for the next few days allowing her relatively easy birds. Heather is good terrain for working a dog, the handler can watch the dog all the time and the dog learns to get her head down.

I do not carry a gun but for those who do, it is wise to accustom a puppy to gunfire before a big day. Some puppies are nervous of the weapon swung to the shoulder more than the report of the gun. Carry a stick and occasionally bring it up as though to fire. Taking the youngster picking-up with an experienced dog has worked well for me so I recommend this procedure. Resist being in a hurry to give the young dog retrieves, she will benefit by being allowed several days just keeping at heel and watching all that is going on. If your dog is going to be a gun's assistant then I strongly advise you to give up several days shooting and to pick-up with the puppy. It really is worth

Picking-up on a grouse moor will give both handler and dog confidence at the start of a shooting session

sacrificing a few days to concentrate wholly on the young dog. Be careful to pick the retrieves carefully, never sending her for anything complicated, or, too easy. Two or three retrieves nicely accomplished are all you should give her and if easy birds fall in the open, temptingly close, leave her on Sit and go and pick them yourself. The first few days under battle conditions will ideally be an extension of your lessons in the home paddock. Personally, I do not like to send a young dog for a freshly shot rabbit or hare until full confidence is gained on live game. A wounded, screaming coney is very upsetting and having once seen a keen young flatcoat retriever completely put off by being sent out for a leveret which shrieked and struggled, I prefer to settle only for partridge, pheasant, pigeon or grouse for the first lesson. Much will depend upon the pupil's character and confidence. Last season my young labrador marked a woodcock, I sent her for it and she picked it nicely. But she has never been hesitant about retrieving anything at all. One of the commonest mistakes is to push the dog along when everything is going well, because it is tempting to give a promising dog too much to do. This is why I like to take a young one in company with a veteran. Apart from the discipline and invaluable education for the youngster watching someone else doing the work, you can then pick your easy unseen ones for the pup; never the birds lying out in the open. If this is not possible, it may be that you can go and stand with a picker-up and let your novice watch the form. If you are going to use your dog in the beating line, keep her beside you for the first few days until she gets accustomed to the noise, the scuttling birds, the glorious smells and the heady atmosphere generated inside the covert by a line of enthusiastic beaters and dogs.

Make a rule not to send the young dog for a bird unless you have definitely marked it down. Helpful dogless guns who tell you that they have a bird down 'over there in the next field' are not, in fact, offering constructive work at all. These cripples and doubtful retrieves should be left for the experienced dogs. It is disheartening for a pup to seek fruitlessly. She has not the experience to know that you really believe there is a bird to be found and there is the risk she will begin to lift her head and plunge about looking for her retrieve, rather than sniffing for it. When this happens, go back to hiding dummies in the long grass and hedgerows on home territory until she gets her nose down again. Continual repetition of the command Hi-lost and accompanying encouraging noises will distract the dog. Moreover, she will be made to look foolish and inefficient. If you are confident that the

Never give a young dog a difficult return like this one if it can be avoided

bird is a dead one and the dog has her head down, working correctly, then leave her to concentrate and, hopefully, she will solve her own problem.

We have all seen enthusiastic owners sending their newly trained dogs for runners and beaming with delight when the dog comes back triumphant. But a strong running cock can be a recipe for disaster to an excitable young dog. A cock pheasant can run like the devil and shows plenty of fight at the end of it. A young dog can hardly be blamed if she crunches a bird which is scratching her nose with his claws, beating her face with his wings and struggling furiously. She really does not know how else to cope with the fury. A youngster of any breed, not just the small ones like spaniels, can crunch the ribs of a retrieve under these circumstances. So, anticipate this problem, avoid putting your dog into a compromising situation and leave the runners to the veterans. Apart from anything else, a runner is an unsteadying influence for any newly trained gundog. Some puppies hold onto their retrieves, reluctant to give up their delicious prize. One of my spaniels always did this on the first day of a new season and I used to worry that she was developing a hard mouth with her jaws clenching the bird whilst she grinned ecstatically in front of me. However, after the initial retrieve she returned to form and no permanent damage was done.

If things do go wrong on the first day, and your pupil makes a mess of things when you first send her about her business in earnest, much as Mel did in the first chapter of this book when Tom sent her out, do not immediately panic and put on the lead. Keep the dog beside you and let her watch what is going on and, if a suitable opportunity presents itself, give her another easy retrieve well away from the other dogs and people. If an opportunity does not arise, resist the temptation to try something which is not completely straightforward. Puppies easily forget and probably no damage has been done, but it is important not to confuse her and to go home chastened and unhappy. If the problem is rank disobedience, then it is back to strict discipline on the lawn at home. The fault is entirely your own because the puppy must not go out shooting until she is thoroughly drilled in obedience and you are sure of her trust in you. There is a world of difference between a young dog which disobeys because it is confused or frightened and one which turns a deaf ear. In either case, you have probably been too hasty in taking your pupil out shooting.

CHAPTER ELEVEN

Problems – Serious and Minor

A gun, or a picker-up, with a young dog which disappoints on her first few outings in public, will likely have sleepless nights worrying about the problem. This will be especially the case if the individual has trained the dog himself. If the dog has been trained professionally then at least he can consult the expert, if he has done the work himself, he will wonder where he has gone wrong.

In nine cases out of ten the problem will be resolved and a year later it will all be forgotten. If the novice trainer is puzzled and cannot see what to do to get things right then he must abandon his text book and seek experienced advice. Never be afraid to ask for help. You will readily be given it and your problem will then be who to listen to! On every shoot there is at least one man, or woman, in the line of guns or in the ranks of the pickers-up and beaters whose dog works quietly and correctly. Don't listen to advice from the rank and file but ask this individual what he suggests that you do. If you do not like his advice or do not feel that you can carry it out with conviction then find an experienced trainer in the neighbourhood and take yourself and your errant dog to him for guidance. This is a pessimistic view and it is most unlikely that any dog, chosen on the lines suggested, and trained by a thoughtful amateur will need such corrective treatment. Certainly, she will not if she has been to a good trainer and you have followed his suggested follow-up training programme. The danger is that a momentary lapse can escalate into a bad habit and so it is really a question of preventative measures and knowing what to guard against.

The commonest fault seen in the ranks of amateur gun dogs in the shooting field is running-in. A keen young dog during her first season may be excused the occasional lapse whilst gaining experience. It is not always possible to pick a straight forward retrieve because all sorts of unforeseen things may happen. A dead bird can erupt into a lively

There is always one man or woman on every shoot whose dogs work quietly and correctly. Ask for advice

Give the miscreant a good shaking, never a thrashing

runner, a miscreant retriever may pinch the bird from under your dog's nose or your enthusiastic pupil may anticipate an order and slip off unbidden about her business. These situations happen to the best of us and handled immediately and firmly no permanent damage will be done. Anticipate trouble, take steps to prevent it and it will not get a chance to happen. A young dog which runs in, or chases, will not learn if she is thrashed on return. Go right out and catch her at it and give her a good shaking, not a thrashing. Then take good care that she does not ever get a second chance. This is an opportunity to use that word No, put her on Sit beside you and when a bird crumples in sight and she raises herself in anticipation put her down again and say No! Use discretion if she is very keen and let her do without another retrieve until she has relaxed and is back with you on that invisible cord again. If vigilance and discipline are always your criterion for every day of the dog's working life then you will have a reliable retriever and she will not run-in, because she will never have tasted the joys of illicit chasing, breaking rules or turning a deaf ear to master.

A dog which picks a bird and then drops it within yards and races off to collect another, is in my humble opinion not fit to be on the shooting field. If any pupil of mine did this, she would be put straight back to the most elementary retrieving in the home paddock. It is sad to see a dog doing this and it is a result of the animal being taken out amongst live falling birds too early – a mixture of misplaced enthusiasm and excitment for the dog and lenience on the part of her owner/trainer. If your dog shows any sign of doing this when you send her out on a retrieve, then take a long look at your training schedule and do not take her out again under battle conditions again until she understands the drill. A dog which messes about with his retrieves is a natural retriever spoiled by wrong handling. When your dog picks a bird, her instinct and training will have instilled in her that she must return to base with her quarry despite any temptation or provocation.

Young dogs seldom do wrong, it is the experienced ones which get slack, along with their handlers. You can never relax with an intelligent gundog, he or she will soon learn the game and enjoy it as much as you do. But you are the boss and must always set the pace. That invisible thread must not be broken – so long as it remains intact there will be no serious problems.

Silence is golden at the covert side, we can discipline our own shrill tones to the drill but it is a different matter when the dog we have at heel begins making a noise. I notice that training books have little helpful to say on the subject because no reliable cure has been found for the culprit who has begun to be vocal. Along with hard mouth, it is a cardinal sin and always puts paid to any competitors chances in a field trial.

At every major shoot which we attend during the season, there is at least one dog which whimpers and whines at master's peg. Every trainer to whom it is mentioned will know about this habit and will certainly have had noisy dogs through the kennel. No trainer would take on a dog which yelped in frustration when dummies or pheasants fell tantalisingly about him. The dog may sit tight but if he makes a noise about it then no one will want him. The habit will already have become too deep-rooted to eradicate. A noisy shooting dog is an appalling nuisance, upsetting the concentration of all guns within earshot and reducing his owner to frustration and despair.

My eleven year-old springer spaniel made an infernal noise when she had to sit and watch the action. She could not bear not to be getting on at once with the job. This developed with old age and now I do not take her shooting any longer. On the trail of a runner, she is perfectly silent but a friend's dog yelps enthusiastically on runners but is silent when birds are plopping down within yards of him. So the wretched habit takes different dogs in different ways. One school of thought considers the trait hereditary and an excitable, highly strung strain will be more likely to let the side down by becoming vocal. Undoubtedly, the habit will be acclerated if other dogs are along too and they get what the culprit considers to be the lion's share of the retrieving work. A whiner will soon consider that he should be allowed all the work and will show his frustration if he does not get it. It may be against the nature of the working spaniel to sit still for long periods but many of them learn to do it. However, where noise is concerned, spaniels are not the only culprits – other gundog breeds can be vocal too. I do believe that 'making a noise' is catching and would not take an impressionable dog out shooting with one which had started whining. The presence of a second retriever would not necessarily make the culprit worse but his habit could rub off on his companion.

One reason for the habit starting may be that the dog was over-faced, introduced to game finding and the heady excitment of a big day prematurely, and was not sufficiently steady and mature to accept the work with equanimity. If it is not immediately corrected, the frustrated dog will soon become unaware that she is whining or squeaking and efforts to stop her will be a waste of time. I remember a nice weimeraner which panted and slavered all the time his master was preparing his meal and he really was not aware of the fuss he was making.

A young dog can usually be reduced to silence by a steely glare and a growl No. The human eye has a strong corrective influence. Again, like other faults, prevention is better than cure and the secret is not to allow the habit to start. Handlers and trainers offer mixed advice with little conviction. Slap or tap the dog's nose as soon as the whining starts, put an eye shield on the dog during the drive or have a companion ready to squirt the dog's muzzle with a soda siphon. Drastic measures, difficult to carry out and do they really work? I rather doubt it, one cannot cart accessories around to fit the crime.

Hard mouth means the dog crushes, or bites, the bird he retrieves. A ghastly crime but not a common one and, like whining, a habit which may develop with old age so it will be incurable and the pensioner retired from active service. A very young dog can handle his game roughly once or twice or clench the bird excitedly before giving it up but rarely will this continue. Take the retrieve away carefully, never grabbing or pulling it from his mouth. Likewise, avoid two dogs going out for the same retrieve or a tug-of-war could result. During the course of every season we usually witness one of these scenes. Never allow children to throw anything at all for the gundogs because careless handling and slackness in delivery is inevitable and could make for biting and the beginning of a hard mouth syndrome.

CHAPTER TWELVE

Thoughts on Beating

Every year, from August until January, the services of efficient beaters are in demand on shoots all over the country. The guns cannot operate without an organisation to show the birds, and fit men and women, with or without reliable dogs are welcome. However, with unemployment offering an inducement to holiday jobs in some areas beating is popular work and the old lags do tend to stay on year after year leaving few spaces in the ranks. Pay may be around nine pounds a day, or just goodwill and a brace of pheasants, and it can take time for a novice to join a team. Start with helping friends, concentrate on learning what the game is all about and leave your dog behind until she is well-trained enough to accompany you.

No keeper will have too many good beaters but ladies who chatter in shrill tones and thus frighten off the birds or who bring dogs which rampage fifty yards ahead of the line in covert will not be asked to join the company again. The work becomes simplified, and more interesting, as one learns the geography of the coverts, gets to know the natives and where game is likely to be hidden. Simple in theory and satisfying when experience has brought a degree of expertise, but more difficult to practise than some beginners appreciate. Beating work starts on the grouse moors, continues with partridges at the back end of September, graduates to full-scale covert shooting from late October until Christmas and then there will be final thinning-out rough days in January.

Head keepers are the men to make up to for beating work because it is they, and not their employers, who arrange beaters. In theory, the same goes for picking-up but, occasionally, the landowner, agent or shoot manager may invite efficient friends to come and pick-up.

Grouse have become big business and with clients paying high rents the moors must be efficiently staffed by responsible loaders, flankers, pickers-up and beaters if a good show of birds is going to be put over the guns. It is marvellous experience to work on a good moor and it is not a question of asking favours here, beaters are always in demand. From beating, a keen man, or woman, with a good gundog may be able to graduate to picking-up and there is no finer school in which to educate a young retriever or working spaniel than on a grouse moor. Beating grouse is not the same as for pheasants, the walking can be arduous and tiring and it can be exhaustingly warm, especially if the heather is long in places. Blisters can result from new boots unless they have been well broken in beforehand. Many beaters favour trainers for walking in heather if the weather is hot. A lightweight cagool or nylon mackintosh with a hood which rolls up into a small bundle is essential because a waxed jacket is too heavy to walk in all day during August or early September.

A good keeper will place his team strategically on a grouse moor and ensure that the drives go smoothly with the minimum of shouting and flag waving. The majority of moors provide the beaters with flags but some people prefer to take their own. Dogs must be impeccably behaved. One of our daughters worked as a beater on a local moor and coped well but she was a strong well-built sixteen year old and lived near enough to come home to a comfortable billet in the evenings. She felt that many girls might find walking in line too exhausting and I think that she is right. Usual arrangements on large grouse moors are for beaters to be housed in an army-style hut with primitive beds and dormitory type lay-out, so there is usually no provision here for girls. On the moor in Scotland where our sons have been working, students from a local university are employed as well as schoolboys old enough to fend for themselves away from home. Twenty boys sleep and mess together. Basic cooking facilities are provided and one young man volunteers to stay behind each day and work as cook for the company. Parents under the misapprehension that some sixteen and seventeen year olds are incapable of looking after themselves after a hard day's work would be surprised at how well they can cope. A moor that I work on in Northumberland, provides a cook and a hot evening meal for resident beaters and there is, therefore, no shortage of recruits here.

The head keeper will tell you what the form is regarding living and feeding arrangements for beaters. Booking for beaters on grouse is usually per week, not per day and obviously long stays of several weeks are encouraged. A keeper organising staff for a two or three

There is always a demand for beaters on the grouse moors

Beaters waiting at the start of a pheasant drive

week grouse let likes to be certain that he has beaters who know the form and who will not let him down by going to the wrong place, lagging behind or turning up late.

Beating for partridges is interesting and less strenuous than for grouse. Drives are short and often over pasture or stubble, but beaters must be very quiet. Partridges do not fly far, but they are scary birds and a covey will swoop off into the next field at the sound of a human voice or someone whistling loudly for a dog. Partridges are nice birds to retrieve and a few days picking-up is very valuable in the early part of the shooting season. Retrieves are seldom long or difficult and the birds are small and make a comfortable mouthful. Very good experience for a young dog.

Many shooting men will assume that the number of pheasants flying over their heads represent all those in covert but the beaters inside know better. There are certain pheasant coverts where a considerable number of birds may not be shown, due to poor work or placing of beaters. The keeper who understands the art of driving and the management of his various drives will save his beaters' legs and will be better able to deploy his forces with advantage. Beaters may appear willing and enthusiastic but do not appreciate being sent on unnecessary detours. Rides and tracks cut through impenetrable coverts are much appreciated and allow us to do our job without too much damage to the extremities. The keeper's voice in the middle of the line is the only one that need regularly be heard although every beater in thick cover should keep in touch with the man on either side of him and this will usually have to be by voice. Chattering and gossiping tends to encourage wily birds to squat and run, rather than take wing. Beaters must be aware that when a group of pheasants is flushed, the whole line must pause. Too many birds over the guns at once is unsatisfactory, especially on a shoot where there are no loaders so beaters must take care not to flush too many at once. The steady advance of a well spaced level line of beaters, keeping up a continuous tapping, with several thorough working dogs will achieve good results and show birds to advantage. As one learns the geography of the coverts it is a great pleasure to visit the same shoots year after year and to compare game seen with previous excursions.

Take a strong stick for beating out bramble bushes and wear sensible waterproof clothing. The role of the humble beater is to show sport for the guns but there are, alas, a few sportsmen who could with advantage consider us too, although to be fair, this applies only to a few ignorant men, of whom many are foreigners. No one can beat out the end of a drive with confidence if there is a possibility of someone taking a chancy shot and we quickly learn who to avoid! With 'let' days now normal practice on many shoots it is prudent to be careful with new guns.

Walking through kale, oilseed rape, roots and game crops take a slightly zig-zag line to and fro, because pheasants can squat between the ranks of beaters who easily walk over them. If you have a good spaniel she will be valuable here, feathering to right and left within a twenty yard radius as you walk. Cast the dog out, using the toot 'turn' note on the whistle if necessary. A good spaniel quarters naturally, but the skill will need practice so that dog and trainer get accustomed to working together. When a bird rises, insist that the dog sits or stops immediately. This also breaks concentration and gives opportunity for another turn. If your dog is not totally reliable keep her at heel or you risk being asked to leave her at home which would be a pity, because an amateur gundog handler is not going to enjoy himself if his dog has to be left in the kennel when he has committed himself to beating on a shoot for the season.

If you pick up a fallen bird during or after a drive, tell the keeper or a picker-up that you found it. Do not allow your dog to begin hoovering about the guns' pegs for birds unless specifically asked to do so. Don't hang about, gossiping to guns, hangers-on or fellow beaters at the end of each drive but keep your ears open for orders and set off smartly for the next drive with the rest of your party. No keeper will have time for rounding up stragglers. If you have your dog beside you, and I hope that you will, then your attention will be amply taken up between watching her and organising yourself. Spaniels which are kept primarily to work as members of a beating team should strictly not be permitted to retrieve. This is how the men who work a team of spaniels manage so efficiently because if the dog has not learnt to pick a bird then there will be no tendency to run-in to shot. However, most amateur handlers would find this impractical because it is seldom that circumstances allow us to keep several dogs for different purposes and few of us get enough work to justify this. My spaniels have always been dual-purpose but it is important to guard against the dog in the beating line pottering or forging ahead on ground scents. Rabbits are now back in our countryside in abundance and are a great nuisance in covert. The idea is for the dogs to find the birds by body scent and not by hunting a line.

Working two dogs in the beating line is much more demanding than picking-up with two or more behind the guns. The latter is relatively straight-forward. Jealousy between members of a working team can be a problem with the younger dog quickly learning to play follow-my-leader, getting his head up or, worse, giving up trying to work at all. A novice with a steady dog which works well in covert should resist the temptation to take on a second pupil unless the handler has had several seasons' experience.

Not the least interesting thing about beating on a shoot, either large or small is the illuminating insight it gives into both sides of a day's shooting. The attitude of the respective guns is interesting because they are enjoying the fruits of the day's labours. Much can be learnt about etiquette and good manners by an observant and interested novice. It is also refreshing to meet individuals who are new to field sports who have become involved as beaters and who have learnt that helping on a shoot does not necessarily mean accepting a supporting role as aides to blood-thirsty sportsmen. Shooting things can help to conserve wildlife rather than destroy it and once you get to know the countryside you can understand this. When it comes to learning at first hand about preserving wildlife, encouraging it to breed and adapt to local conditions and the delicate balance which must be maintained between game and predators there is no better place to go than on a beating line at a shoot. Here, you will rub shoulders with men who have spent a lifetime on the land. No one denies that there are conflicting interests between agriculture and field sports. You may get a jaundiced view from some of the old hands but you can also draw your own conclusions at first hand.

CHAPTER THIRTEEN

Picking-up

It is time now to graduate from the beating line to the exciting task of working as a picker-up. It is possible to be invited onto an estate after accompanying a husband, friend or relation who was carrying a gun and could not manage his dog as well. Invitations to pick-up come strictly from shoot owners or head keepers and not from syndicate or guest guns. Picking-up has become a sport in itself and work on big shoots is much sought after. If you are fortunate enough to have been invited to help in this capacity always remember that it is the guns who call the tune. The majority of them have paid a great deal of money to enable the show to go on at all and they will not take kindly to a picker-up sending his, or her dog in to collect the birds which they have shot, and which they rightly consider are their own dog's property. Moreover, there is sure to be a veteran picker-up who will be weighing up the new recruit, so respect him and his knowledge of the estate and its management.

A good picker-up must study form. Arrive before time at the meeting place and if you need to ask the keeper the programme for the day then allow time for this before he gets involved with his boss and the guests. If there is a veteran picker-up, then put yourself in his hands and do not bother the keeper or the shoot manager with questions. He will probably keep the likely hot spots for himself and give you the dud ones but birds are unpredictable and always keep one guessing. Too often no one seems to be in charge so the ground is sometimes covered in haphazard fashion and, depending upon wind and the way the birds flew last time over, the drives can be changed disconcertingly without any directions to a new recruit. We are generally assumed to be thought readers and to know the plans without having to ask. After several seasons on a shoot it is rewarding to have learnt every drive and to know instinctively where to go to make yourself useful.

Ask the keeper the programme for the day before he gets involved with the guns

Leave the dog, or dogs, in your car until you are in a position to watch them when they are let out to join the company at the meeting place. It is bad manners to allow them to relieve themselves on your host's lawn or in his yard or to potter off into the shrubbery when you cannot give your attention to controlling them. By midday an early breakfast begins, or rather ceases, to tell but it is prudent to resist liberal resource to the cherry brandy proffered by a kind host or a friendly gun. The wind may be biting and the frost keen, but it is a golden rule that you must keep your wits about you and your voice in low key. The picker-up does a very useful job but he, or she, must remember the rules and stick to them. Unless specifically invited to join lunch in barn, bothy or house by the host, bring your own bait and put it in a portable packet suitable for the pocket in case transport is unreliable or not provided. It probably will be, but it takes one or two sorties on a new shoot to learn the form. It is prudent not to be parted from one's victuals or you find yourself sponging on someone else, or going all day without nourishment. A bad start for a novice working on a new shoot.

Having settled where you are going to stand during a drive do not wander about. This is disconcerting for the guns who are watching for birds ahead and to right and left, and can hardly be expected to watch out for a foolish picker-up scurrying about behind them. Put your dog on Sit and keep your eyes and ears open marking every bird that comes down to the best of your ability, but do not move. Never send a dog out to collect unless you are absolutely confident that he will keep his mind on the job in hand. Collecting birds during a drive is permissible in certain circumstances, but use discretion here. If a cock pheasant hits the ground with a thud and then picks itself up and streaks for the nearest forbidden covert which you know to be full of young birds, then it is good sense to send out a reliable dog. Stay silent, put your trust in the dog's ability to collect with minimum fuss, and busy yourself marking the other cripples which are planing down well back behind the line. Experience will bring confidence marking birds, noting contours of hillock, ditch and scree and being able to go straight to the fall when the drive is over. Even a few birds mustered and brought to hand bring confidence to both handler and dog. Some pickers-up take home ten pounds at the end of the day. Good amateurs who expect nothing more than the occasional brace of birds for the pot and are satisfied with only the privilege of working their dogs in lovely surroundings are now in demand and with shoot costs so high, it is easy to see why.

There is sure to be a veteran picker-up already working on the shoot

Watch carefully during the first drive which guns have dogs and this will set the pattern for the rest of the day. No host wants expensively produced birds left out as food for foxes, so wounded birds and those which fall well back behind the line are the ones that we must go after. Occasionally, a picker-up is asked to act as a stop in the pheasant covert or as a flanker on the grouse moor. A nice change and a chance to enjoy the terrain especially on grouse driving days. It is also valuable for the dog to remain static and watch birds falling and other dogs working. Towards the end of the season it may be necessary to join in with the beaters. Be sure that the dogs do not take advantage of this game-finding task. Once a picker-up's dog gets its head down and starts to hunt and flush rather than seeking to retrieve, he can quickly get out of hand.

Time between drives must not be spent socialising with guns. A picker-up who is doing his or her job properly will be busy looking for the slain or at least comparing notes with the other picker-up. If a few birds have to be left out, tell the head keeper where you think they may be and he will try and collect next day. Planning and co-operation between keepers, pickers-up and beaters can be lamentable on a few shoots so you will have to keep your wits about you and, sticking to these guidelines, make yourself useful without fuss.

On the grouse moor it is customary to stand about one hundred and fifty yards behind the butts. With pheasant and partridges pickers-up are generally closer but it is a common fault to crowd too close to the guns to be near the action. This is not only dangerous but worrying for the right-minded gun. I received a pellet on my cheek once which taught me a lesson. It was on the grouse moor and the fault was entirely mine.

Finally, always thank the host at the end of the day for allowing you to come and help pick-up. The days when head keepers and veteran pickers-up could behave like prima donnas are over. They no longer call the tune. Todays harsh economics dictate that landowners and paying guns, whether a syndicate or a visiting group, spend a great deal of money to provide a good shoot and those who come to help should regard it as a privilege to be invited to do so.

CHAPTER FOURTEEN

The Gun's Dog

The dog which accompanies the man or woman who carries a gun may look as though he has an easy time of it but, in reality, I think his job is difficult and it is not surprising that many guns find it difficult to control a dog as well as to shoot. Temptations abound. On a big shoot, birds fall practically at the dog's feet and an intelligent canine soon learns that momentarily his master's attention is not solely on him. No wonder so many take advantage and have to be secured to stakes stuck in the ground. Moreover, continually retrieving birds lying in the open, which a good shot usually has around him, is not conductive to educating a youngster who risks the temptation to begin rushing about looking for his birds rather than getting his nose down to scent them. Hopefully, the gun's dog will become adept at marking his master's birds and will have every opportunity to do so. Many shoots alternate guns standing and walking on drives and the young dog must be kept to heel and not allowed to flush birds because this will otherwise accelerate a tendency to run in.

For a first season dog, it really is wise for the gun to apply much of his attention to his dog rather than his shooting. Allowances will have to be made, especially if the man has been accustomed to having an experienced gundog at his side. It may be possible to work the dog for half a day and confine it to the car whilst shooting in the afternoon. Forays on the rough shoot will have to be carefully monitored too. Leave beating out the hedgerows and the brambles to the old hands. Gathering duck after evening or morning flighting is good practice for a youngster and many young dogs do this well with no detriment to their education. Sitting quietly at master's side in the dusk and then finding the quarry in the reeds is good practice and can only be achieved by using nose, not eyes. The dog will, of course, have been introduced already to swimming. Hopefully, he will not need to do

Many gun's dogs are to be seen tied to stakes in the ground

this for his first half dozen retrieves. An intelligent dog will soon learn to listen for the duck coming in. Avoid sending the dog to the fall immediately or you could risk encouraging him to run in, but do not keep him waiting more than a few minutes. Duck, especially cripples, falling into marshes or shallow water need to be quickly collected. The dog will learn to differentiate between flighting and formal shooting and these excursions do build a good relationship. It is all good experience.

Invitations to shoot may, or may not, include the gun's dog. If it is to be a 'big' day, leave a young dog at home because shooting well requires skill and full concentration. There is now a new trend towards the 'roving' syndicate, a definite change from the conventional form of resident group membership which has had a monopoly for so many years. A travelling syndicate initially appoints one member to be the organiser and it is his responsibility to arrange days on different estates. Many shoots have given up a syndicate team and concentrate entirely on offering 'let' days. The organiser will shop around the neighbourhood and contact landowners and/or keepers to make arrangements. Current lets for pheasant or partridges run at an average

Leave a goose for an experienced dog to collect

twelve pounds a bird, and a good shoot will offer one hundred, one hundred and fifty or two hundred bird days. Estates which offer walked-up rough shooting are popular, especially with parties of clients domiciled in the south where rough shooting is now almost non-existent in some areas. Sixty to eighty pounds a day is the average rate, with duck flighting thirty pounds and goose flighting forty pounds. These are 1986–7 current market rates. The usual arrangement is a brace of birds per gun included in the fee and the option to buy more at prevailing market rates.

It is important for the travelling syndicate to appoint a conscientious member of the team to act as organiser. Landowners are looking for ways to make their shooting days attractive and competitive compared to what the neighbours offer. The organiser should take the trouble to visit estates, to see the drives and the stands offered and then the team have a better chance of value for money and an enjoyable day. Some estates offer drinks and lunch in the package. Others may provide soup at midday or be willing to allow clients to bring their own picnics. Most are flexible and try to make their guests feel welcome. The travelling syndicate has the advantage of being spared any regular commitment regarding the running of a shoot and has no responsibility for employing a keeper, supplying and maintaining birds or fixing up beaters, pickers-up or loaders. It may not be a substitute for the man or woman who enjoys a commitment to his shoot but it does have appeal to the gun who likes a bit of variety.

It always surprises me that more guns on these 'travelling' syndicates do not bring their dogs with them. I pick up on an estate which now hosts predominately let days and the guns often remark that they have a good dog which they left behind because they did not know if it would be welcome. In fact, the guns call the tune and it is their day. A telephone call is all that is necessary to enquire if a dog, or dogs, would be acceptable and, on some estates, they would be, provided that they are mature and disciplined. An obedient working dog which accompanies a gun will be acceptable on any shoot, however many other resident dogs there are likely to be.

CHAPTER FIFTEEN

Bringing a Young Dog On: Pro's and Con's of Breeding

Picking-up, and beating, on several pheasant shoots averaging one hundred and fifty to two hundred bird days at the height of the season, I have not found it strictly necessary to use two dogs. A fit dog working alone should be able to cover the work on her own provided she is not expected to do so on consecutive days too frequently. With an immature dog or an elderly one, however, you will need a second retriever. On the grouse moor it is an advantage to have two, in fact, provided you can manage them, I think that three are not too many. When picking-up the dog must be self-reliant, ranging wide and often having to use her own initiative to investigate likely corries and slopes where maimed birds may lie. The handler cannot cover the work by continually handling the dog on to her retrieves with grouse. So it will be exhausting work for one dog especially in hot weather.

A reliable mature retriever can teach a youngster a great deal by example. Keep the pup at heel and let her watch her mentor at work, not for one or two drives, but for several days. There is nothing like it for teaching a youngster what the game is all about. You cannot keep the pup at heel too long provided the older dog is obedient and works correctly to hand. A good example will be first class initiation to battle conditions in the field. If the young dog is allowed to go out on a retrieve too early she will not only follow the old dog, but can easily start to race about in competition. The older one will be jealous and could also begin to deteriorate. Select easy retrieves for the puppy and try to give her these whilst the experienced one is already out on a more difficult retrieve. Hopefully, the youngster will have found hers and brought it to hand before the old one has returned with the elusive cripple. Keep these guidelines in mind and be satisfied with the young dog achieving one or two nice retrieves each time out, so that she gains confidence and develops a style of her own without trying to follow her sibling.

A diffident pup can gain confidence from a leader if she is reluctant to face heavy cover. This lesson must be taught on training walks, never in the shooting field or it will simply degenerate into follow-my-leader. I had a young spaniel which had to learn to face brambles and overgrown ditches which abound on our rough shoots here and, although an enthusiastic and stylish retriever of her dummies in the open, she was reluctant to enter thick cover. At that time, my husband had a very good labrador, a small stylish bitch whose greatest joy was plunging into thick undergrowth. She was just like a tough spaniel and adored rough shooting, flushing birds or ground game from blind ditches and gorse bushes with great flair. She taught my little spaniel by example. I used to throw the dummy into cover and the youngster would teeter on the edge with her eyes popping out of her head in amazement as the old dog bull-dozed her way in and then came out triumphant, tail wagging away as though the whole exercise had been enormous fun. Quite soon the spaniel could not resist joining in and thereafter soon found that the operation was not only bearable but rewarding.

Spring is in the air – the young bitch will soon be coming in season and what fun it would be to have a litter of puppies tumbling about on the lawn. Moreover, now that she has had a full season of work, the bitch is doing really well and looks like being first class. Surely it would be an idea to keep the line on by breeding another good one? There should be plenty of buyers for the pups judging by the praise the bitch earned for her work and we can keep the best one for ourselves . . .

Is it really a good idea as soon as a good young dog has got his, or her, act together to have another youngster to bring on? I have seen so many amateur handlers succumb to the temptation of having a successor to their prodigy far too soon, with the result that, within eighteen months, the handler is attempting to introduce another novice to work before the first one has had a fair chance to prove herself. The result too often is two mediocre gundogs instead of one first-class one. Very few amateurs can make a good job of two novice dogs at different stages of training and experience when much of the work must be done in the field. Is it really wise, or necessary, to breed as soon as the dog is two or three years old? Surely better to give the dog another year or two and to enjoy a well-disciplined useful dog,

Fun to have puppies tumbling about on the lawn

apart from the opportunity to assess whether the animal is really worth breeding from. Far too many mediocre dogs are being bred. Friends often ask me if I know anyone wanting a gundog pup because they have one or two left-overs from a litter for which to find homes. These used to be chiefly labradors, now there seem to be almost as many spaniels on offer. No doubt they may be promising pups, but there is simply not the demand for the numbers being bred.

Some bitches have large litters. A neighbour of ours had nine dogs to find homes for and after sleepless nights and weeks of expensive advertising she had to give the last two away. Neither of these went to shooting homes and one unfortunately turned into a roaming nuisance in his village. Potential gundog owners are discerning and take great care to choose a puppy with an impeccable background. So unless you are certain of good homes for the puppies do not be tempted to breed from your bitch. It is surprising how many buyers fade away when puppies materialise. Moreover, unless a bitch is really sound, biddable and intelligent at her work, it is wrong to breed with a view to selling the progeny as shooting companions.

One good puppy should sell for about sixty pounds at eight to ten weeks. It now costs thirty pounds to advertise in a local paper, and more in a national one, and the cost of rearing (without veterinary

Very few teenagers have time to train a gundog

expenses) can run into hundreds of pounds. So breeding a litter of gundogs is not a lucrative sideline. It might be wiser, and it will certainly be cheaper and have more guarantee of success, to buy in a puppy with first class credentials at eight to ten weeks old, having previously seen the parents working. This system has worked well for me.

Parents do sometimes wish to give a keen boy or girl a dog of their own to train, but the moral here is not to give the child a puppy until he or she is ready to take a responsible interest in owning one. Teenage children have a lot of pressure during school terms and they need to be fairly dedicated to want to take on a young gundog.

Moreover, it is not easy for a boy to handle a dog in the field as well as trying to learn to shoot well at the same time. We only need to look around at the gundogs staked down beside their adult owners out shooting, to know that their fathers do not find it very easy. If you do give a young person a gundog puppy, a good idea is to encourage attendance at local training classes. There are good ones being organised in most localities and a boy or girl can take more kindly to being told what to do by an outsider than by a parent. It will be good discipline for the young handler as well as the puppy.